ISBN 978-1-5281-9898-1
PIBN 10965858

1 MONTH OF
FREE
READING

at
www.ForgottenBooks.com

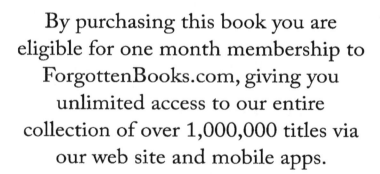

By purchasing this book you are eligible for one month membership to ForgottenBooks.com, giving you unlimited access to our entire collection of over 1,000,000 titles via our web site and mobile apps.

To claim your free month visit:
www.forgottenbooks.com/free965858

CITY PLANNING IN THE SOUTH:
THE FINDINGS AND RECOMMENDATIONS OF THE
SOUTHERN REGIONAL CONGRESS ON CITY PLANNING

A 55-636

August 17-19, 1953
Roanoke, Virginia.

Howard K. Menhinick
Chairman, Congress Steering Committee

Leo J. Zuber
Congress Director

Richard H. Leach
Editor, Congress Proceedings

Southern Regional Education Board
830 West Peachtree Street, N.W.
Atlanta, Georgia

January, 1954

STEERING COMMITTEE FOR THE SOUTHERN REGIONAL CONGRESS ON CITY PLANNING

Members of the Regional Committee on City Planning

George F. Gant, Consultant for Graduate Programs, Southern Regional Education Board

Leonard M. Logan, Director, Institute of Community Development, University of Oklahoma

Howard K. Menhinick, Regents' Professor of City Planning, Georgia Institute of Technology

John A. Parker, Head, Department of City and Regional Planning, University of North Carolina

Members of the Advisory Committee on City Planning

Frederick J. Adams, Head, Department of City and Regional Planning, Massachusetts Institute of Technology

Walter H. Blucher, Executive Director, American Society of Planning Officials

John Gaus, Professor of Government, Littauer Center, Harvard University

James W. Martin, Director, Bureau of Business Research, University of Kentucky

Harold V. Miller, Executive Director, Tennessee State Planning Commission

The Congress Director

Leo J. Zuber, Assistant Director, Metropolitan Planning Commission, Atlanta, Georgia

Chairmen of The Congress Working Committees

William S. Bonner, Acting Director Social Science Research Division, Institute of Science and Technology, University of Arkansas

Margaret Carroll, Planner, Harlan Bartholomew and Associates

Lawrence L. Durisch, Chief of Government Research, Division of Regional Studies, Tennessee Valley Authority

Gerald Gimre, Executive Director, Nashville Housing Authority

Aelred J. Gray, Chief Community Planner, Government Research Branch, Tennessee Valley Authority

Philip P. Green, Jr., Assistant Director, Institute of Government, University of North Carolina

Philip Hammer, Executive Officer, Committee of the South, Nat'l. Planning Association

George W. Hubley, Jr., Executive Director, Agricultural and Industrial Development Board

Albert Lepawsky, Professor of Political Science, University of Alabama

Buford L. Pickens, Dean, School of Architecture, Washington University

Richard L. Steiner, Director, Baltimore Redevelopment Commission

CONTENTS

CHAPTER I

THE SOUTHERN REGIONAL CONGRESS ON CITY PLANNING

THE SOUTHERN REGIONAL CONGRESS ON CITY PLANNING

The Southern Regional Congress on City Planning was held at Roanoke, Virginia,
August 17, 18, and 19, 1953. Over one hundred people actively engaged in planning
in sixteen states, fifty-two cities and the District of Columbia, constituting
the leadership of the profession in the South, attended the Roanoke Congress.
They came as official representatives of the institutions and agencies most concerned with urban planning and redevelopment in the region: colleges and universities active in some aspect of city planning; official city planning boards,
urban redevelopment commissions, state planning agencies, and federal departments
with an interest in the field; professional societies in planning and allied
fields; businesses and industries with important stakes in the development of
southern cities; foundations concerned with city planning problems; and professional city planning consulting firms. Altogether 82 different institutions
and agencies were represented at the Congress.

Background of Congress

For three days this distinguished group of delegates met to discuss and reach
agreement on the programs and activities in city planning instruction, research
and service which are most urgently needed to secure the orderly development of
the rapidly growing cities of the South. The delegates came together at a time
when the South is experiencing the same rapid urbanization other sections of
the nation felt a generation or so ago. They were confronted with the fact that
between 1940 and 1950 the urban population of the South increased 37.5 per cent,
compared to an increase for the nation as a whole of only 19.5 per cent. To put
it another way, almost the entire population increase in the South in the decade
between 1940 and 1950 was an urban one. Nor does the trend seem to have changed
since 1950. This circumstance, complicated by the greater industrialization and
increased complexity of government which has paralleled the increasing urban development, points to an acute need in the South for trained city planners, who

can use their skill and professional experience to help avoid some of the problems which have accompanied urban growth elsewhere. The purpose of the Congress
was to make possible the formulation of a program of action to meet these problems
in city planning which would reflect the joint experience and knowledge of the
best minds in the field. The results of the delegates' collaborative efforts
comprise the report that follows.

Sponsorship of Congress

The Southern Regional Congress on City Planning was sponsored by the Universities
of North Carolina and Oklahoma, the Georgia Institute of Technology, and the
Southern Regional Education Board. It was specifically the undertaking of the
Regional Committee on City Planning which was established in 1952 by the terms
of a Memorandum of Agreement among the three universities and the Southern Regional
Education Board. These educational institutions have agreed to plan their programs together so that they will complement each other and more effectively serve
the region. The Board, an agency provided for in the Southern Regional Education
Compact among the fourteen southern states, is commissioned "to explore fully,
recommend, where desirable, and develop, where needed, interstate collaboration
in the support, expansion, or establishment of regional services or schools for
graduate, professional and technical education." Under this broad mandate, it
has joined with universities in cooperative action in more than a dozen fields.
City planning is a field of great significance to the region, of high cost, and
of limited student enrollment, and as such, one which is an essential part of the
Board's developing regional education program.

The Regional Committee on City Planning decided to sponsor a Congress as its first
major undertaking. It regards the findings and recommendations of the Congress as
the base on which may be built a series of vigorous programs designed to promote
city planning instruction, research and service in the South.

Advance Preparations for Congress

In order that the delegates to the Congress might make their most effective

contributions, preparations were begun far in advance of the meeting in Roanoke. Several months before the Congress convened, the Regional Committee met in Atlanta with the Advisory Committee on City Planning, and during the course of a two-day meeting chose a Congress Director to make the detailed arrangements for the Congress, decided upon its general purposes, and developed plans for its conduct. It was decided that the Congress should be a strictly working session and that, to make it so, it should be divided into twelve[1] working committees. It was agreed that every delegate should be assigned to one of the committees and that each committee should be given the responsibility for a particular subject and for developing and reporting back to the assembled Congress its specific recommendations for action in the area of its concern. Topics for committee consideration were tentatively agreed upon, and the guiding objectives for each working committee were laid down. Each was to be commissioned to reach general agreement on desirable and achievable objectives, generally within one year's time, in its field of inquiry, and to consider and recommend methods by which those objectives might be accomplished. In particular, it was decided that each committee should be requested to identify those problems, or those phases of its topic, which had regional aspects and to identify those for which a regional organization or approach might appear most useful. In addition, it was decided that while the committees should be exploratory in nature, they should produce at the end of their deliberations a concrete definition of objectives, a program to be achieved, and recommended means of achieving it. Finally, the chairmen of the several working committees were chosen at the initial planning session. Great care was exercised in making these choices, for it was clear that the success of the Congress would largely depend on the effectiveness of the committee chairmen. As soon as agreement had been reached on persons for the several assignments, invitations were

---

1. The work of the twelfth committee, the Committee on Congress Publications, was conceived to be chiefly post-Congress. Thus, it did not function actively at the Roanoke meeting and this report contains no recommendations emanating from it.

extended to them. From that point on, the committee chairmen became an integral part of the planning process, and much of the credit for the outcome of the Congress is due to their hard work in the final months before the Congress met. They, together with the Congress Director, the Regional Committee, and the Advisory Committee, formed the Congress Steering Committee which operated from that time on to make all the final plans for the meeting.

Activities of Congress Steering Committee

The Steering Committee performed four major functions. It prepared a list of the institutions and agencies concerned with city planning in the South and selected from it approximately one hundred which were representative of all important segments of urban planning, to which invitations to name a delegate to the Congress were sent during June and July. It discussed and approved the tentative list of committee topics, making sure that it included the most significant problems facing city planners, and prepared detailed job descriptions for each committee, which the committee chairmen then circulated to serve the members of their committees as guides in their pre-Congress thinking. As replies were received from the invitations extended to institutions and agencies, it assigned the delegates named as nearly as possible to the working committees closest to their interests and training. And finally, it supervised the preparation of a considerable number of working papers which were assembled into a portfolio for distribution to each delegate at the opening of the Congress to provide a quick orientation to the purposes of the Congress and helpful guidance throughout the meeting. The portfolio included a roster of the participants, a statement of the objectives of the Congress and of each committee, the job description of each committee and the related materials the several committee chairmen had assembled to provide their committee members with a sound basis for discussion at the first committee meeting, and two documents prepared by the Regional Committee on City Planning — one, a statement on its proposed cooperative program in city planning instruction, research and service in the South, and the other, a compilation of the existing

activities of southern educational institutions in instruction, research and service in city planning and related fields.[2]

Program of Congress

As the Congress proceeded, the program was so scheduled that committee work received major attention. The Congress opened with a short general session. The Chairman of the Steering Committee, Mr. Menhinick, reminded the delegates of the purposes of the Congress and told them that their sessions might "well mark the starting point of a significant upsurge in urban planning and development in the South that may result in finer cities than our country has ever known before." Dean Lloyd W. Chapin, speaking for the sponsoring organizations, read letters of welcome from the presidents of the three university sponsors and delivered the keynote address.[3] Dr. John E. Ivey, Jr., Director of the Southern Regional Education Board, brought greetings from the fourth sponsor and briefly told the delegates of the concern which motivated the Southern Regional Education Board's interest and activity in the Congress. Leo J. Zuber, Congress Director, concluded the session with instructions on how the Congress would operate. After the opening session, the delegates met for the rest of the day in their respective committees. A second general session was held the morning of the second day. It was designed to acquaint the members of each working committee with the topics and methods of procedure of all the committees. The chairmen of four of the working committees reported on the activity and thinking to date of their own and three other related committees. After each report there was helpful discussion from the floor. Each committee thus obtained the ideas and suggestions of the other delegates.

The second afternoon was devoted again to committee sessions. The preliminary report of each committee was completed late that afternoon. Each was turned over

---

2. The roster is reproduced as an appendix to this report.

3. The body of Dean Chapin's address is given on pp. 8-13 of this report.

to the Steering Committee, which then carefully reviewed and correlated it with
the reports of the other committees. While the Steering Committee was occupied
with its review, the delegates of the Congress met in a third general session
with Carl Feiss, the delegate of the Housing and Home Finance Agency, in the
chair. This session was designed to enable the delegates to evaluate the Congress
as a working device. Because the Southern Regional Education Board regarded the
Congress as a major experiment in methodology, it was keenly interested in having
an assessment of its success. The Board, since its inception, has sought a mechanism by which the states and the institutions and agencies in each of them might
most effectively work together on problems of joint interest. The opinions expressed at the third general session made it clear that a successful first step in
developing techniques for regional collaboration had been devised. With no ex-
ceptions, the delegates who expressed themselves during that meeting were enthusi-
astic about the Congress mechanism. All agreed that the answer to Mr. Feiss'
opening question, "Is a Congress as a device to secure mass working on ideas a
good one?", should be affirmative. Several helpful suggestions for future
Congresses were received: there was some feeling that there could have been more
substance to some of the working committee topics; that the objectives of the ·
Congress could have been better defined; and that not enough stress had been put
on the practical problems facing the profession. The consensus, however, was
that the Congress constituted a good beginning in finding a way to secure better
development of the region's urban resources.

The Congress closed with a general session, the morning of the third day, at
which each committee report and set of recommendations was summarized by the
chairman, discussed, sometimes modified, and finally adopted as the consensus
of the group. Mayor Charles P. Farnsley of Louisville, Kentucky, made the con-
cluding speech of the Congress, in which he urged city planners to embark on a

crusade for the well being of the urban citizens of the South. He suggested the use of "city agents" to work in urban communities as county agents have long worked in rural areas.

The results of the Southern Regional Congress on City Planning, as Dean Chapin remarked in his opening address, "may well have profound and continuing effects upon the future of the cities of the South and its people," for its findings and recommendations come not only at a time of challenge but from the careful and deliberate consideration of men and women who represent the institutions and agencies which must meet that challenge. The recommendations made herein are of signal importance because each recommendation represents the consensus of all the delegates to the Congress. As a consequence, for the first time anywhere in the country, there exists a set of recommendations in the field of city planning which is the product of the considered judgment and reasoning of the persons and agencies most closely concerned with city planning in a major region of the country.

The report that follows is not intended as minutes of the Congress. Its purpose is to present the findings and recommendations of the eleven working committees, with enough additional material to make them meaningful. The recommendations have been edited for uniformity, but stand otherwise as written on the occasion of the Congress.

CHAPTER II

CITY PLANNING IN THE SOUTH: THE CHALLENGE

CITY PLANNING IN THE SOUTH: THE CHALLENGE*

* The following is the main body of the address of <u>Lloyd W. Chapin,</u>
<u>Dean of Faculties, Georgia Institute of Technology,</u> as delivered to
the first general session of the Southern Regional Congress on City
Planning.

It is the hope of the sponsors and the explicit objective of this Congress that
there will be developed here a truly representative program of city planning
instruction, research, and service in the South. To accomplish that purpose there
have been invited from fourteen southern states, extending from Maryland to
Kentucky to Texas, official representatives of educational institutions, and of
state and local planning agencies, and other notable individuals whose joint considerations here will reflect the judgment of the outstanding leaders in city
planning in this southern region. A broadly useful and truly representative program will be concerned with important matters beside the offering of curricula
in city planning at universities, essential as that is. If instruction in city
planning is to be dealt with, the terms should be interpreted to include education not only at the graduate and collegiate level, but in high schools and
elementary schools as well, and in the fields of adult education. The program
should take into account the needs of these southern regions for research in the
field of city planning, together with some consideration of the auspices under
which various types of research projects may be conducted and some exploration of
the possible sources of funds for financing research.

Also within the field of study should be the question of how needed technical city
planning services may be made available, such as through private planning engineers
and consultants, through the joint use of technicians by cities that cannot afford
full-time services, through technical assistance to smaller cities by state
planning agencies, educational institutions, and leagues of municipalities. Perhaps there are other ways which the experience and wisdom of the delegates to the
Congress may bring forward.

In short, this is a working Congress, and the accomplishment of the members of this assembly during these next three days may mark the beginning of an era of accelerated planning in the South.

It is not necessary to emphasize the need and usefulness and timeliness of such a Congress as this. There was a time when the American who sought excitement and adventure went westward with the advancing frontier. Now he needs only to step out of his door and make his daily attempt to reach his office to encounter hazards far more numerous and more deadly than his buckskin-clad great grandfather faced in the primeval forests and prairies. The historians tell us that the American frontier closed in 1892, and now that the wilderness has practically disappeared, cities constitute the new frontiers of adventure for the men and women of today. Cities have their jungles, their well-nigh impenetrable central business districts, their unmarked and almost impassable trails, their cataracts and whirlpools of traffic, and their hazards of automobile ambush. The experienced explorer makes a life-time of conversation from one tall tale of a herd of charging elephants, but the American city dweller faces careening masses of freight trucks, busses, and trolleys by the score every hour. The taming of the city, if you please, and the making of it a place for convenient, healthful and pleasant living offer perhaps one of the greatest adventures of modern civilization and a challenging problem and opportunity.

This is particularly true with respect to the cities in the South, which is rapidly changing from a basically agrarian to an urban culture. This is a result, in large measure, of the mechanization of agricultural workers who are moving to cities, seeking and finding employment in newly developed industries and their accompanying trades and services. For example, in 1920, of the fourteen southern states, only Maryland and Florida had more than 35 per cent of their people living in urban communities; in 1950 only Arkansas, Mississippi, and North Carolina had less than 35 per cent of their people living in urban communities. To put it

another way, in 1920 only Maryland had more than 50 per cent of its population
in urban communities; by 1950 Maryland had been joined by Florida, Louisiana,
Oklahoma, and Texas. And these figures make no allowance for the large number of
urban workers who live in near-by rural areas. Thus, the cities of the South,
both large and small, are entering upon a period of rapid expansion with an urgent
need for leadership in planning their present and future growth so as to avoid
many of the serious mistakes of urban development that have occurred in cities in
the sections of the United States that became highly urbanized at an earlier date,
mistakes that are even now being repeated as our small cities become larger and
our larger cities sprawl through aimless suburban developments: streets too
narrow, jogs and dead-ends, streets too steep or too sharply curved, streets
that cannot be properly drained or served with sewers, house lots too narrow, no
sites reserved for schools, playgrounds, parks or for other required public purposes. Cities have been allowed to develop and are now developing with such
overcrowding of the land, so little open space and greenery, so much ugliness,
noise, and dirt, so much intermingling of business and industry in residential
sections, that people who can do so leave the cities for the surrounding country-
side to find pleasant living conditions. The result is central cities that are
rotting at the core, with downtown districts permitted to become so congested
that people will no longer go to them to do business. The dismal catalog can be
extended almost indefinitely. Extensive slum areas caused by overcrowding of the
land, new schools built in areas that have promptly become business and industrial
districts in which there are no children; sewer and water mains planned and built
and then torn up and replaced and torn up and replaced again; houses, stores,
and factories permitted to locate in low areas subject to periodic flooding with
resulting human misery, economic loss, and costly public expenditure. Miles of
highway frontage blighted by shoe-string business developments and converted into
league after league of ugliness.

It is encouraging to observe today that many of the most progressive steps in
city planning and development are taking place now in the fourteen southern states
represented here. Only a few examples, selected at random from the many notable
planning developments occurring in the South, need be cited to prove the point.
Specially noteworthy is the cooperative program in city planning instruction, research and service of the Southern Regional Education Board under whose auspices
we are meeting today. It has attracted the attention of planners throughout the
nation, east and west. The South has taken a leading position in meeting realistically the governmental problems of metropolitan growth. One may cite Atlanta's
well-known Plan of Improvement and its Metropolitan Planning Commission, the
ability of Virginia's cities to accomplish needed urban annexation, promptly and
equitably by court order, the unique solution of the urban fringe problem at
Baton Rouge, and the move toward the merging of county and city government at
Miami. The many-sided attack of the city of Baltimore upon its urban planning
and development problem merits attention. Comprehensive city and county planning,
public housing, urban redevelopment, and a nationally famous project to eliminate
its most substandard housing conditions through concerted enforcement of building,
housing and sanitation codes are significant elements in this program.

Furthermore, the South is leading in providing planning and development assistance
for smaller communities. The programs developed in this field by the State
Planning Commissions of Tennessee and Alabama are very successful pioneer accomp-
lishments. The State of Virginia has under way a most promising program, as does
the State of Kentucky. These state planning agencies have added to their staff
city planners whose services are made available to the smaller cities of their
state to aid them in the solution of their problems of planning and development.
The result has been the creation of nearly a hundred local planning commissions
which are at work on the problems of developing their small towns into more
attractive, convenient, efficient and pleasant places in which to live. Nor has

his been entirely a governmental activity. In Georgia, the largest public
tility in the state, the Georgia Power Company, has made outstanding contribu-
ions to the improvement of the cities of the state by a program of champion home-
own contests which it has sponsored for the past several years.

hese encouraging achievements are simply a testimonial that the South is at last
ecoming generally aware of the need for intelligent and enlightened planning of
ities, but it is still faced with many unsolved problems in urban planning and
evelopment. Such problems as the steady increase in automobile traffic conges-
ion on streets and highways and the critically short supply of downtown parking
spaces need attention. Transit systems are finding it impossible to render adequate service, with the result that people in increasing numbers are deserting
transit services for their private automobiles, which in turn increase highway
raffic congestion, making it more difficult still for the transit lines to render
rapid service and earn an operating income. This circle leads around again to
still more cars on the streets and to a still greater demand for downtown parking
spaces.

Cities have much to learn in the writing and use of zoning laws. Too frequently
a zoning ordinance is set up to meet a special need, and without a realization
that properly a zoning law should be a device for accomplishing a city plan and
that the plan should be agreed upon first - not the zoning restrictions, which
are by their very nature negative in character. Zoning can prevent improper land
uses, but it cannot positively assure proper land use.

In many cities today slums and blighted areas are spreading more rapidly than they
are being cleared. Rapid and haphazard urban growth and industrialization are
polluting streams, depleting water resources, and wastefully overburdening public
facilities.

This is a set of circumstances to which must be brought intelligence and ingenuity and imagination and diligent effort. It seems quite clear that the cities of these United States have not yet succeeded in becoming truly satisfactory for human occupancy for the vast majority of their residents in terms of beauty, convenience, quiet and healthfulness, and it is only through guidance that many citizens will come to realize - perhaps for the first time - that a city can be so laid out and so built as to be beautiful and convenient and quiet and healthful, and that the ✔ longer such planning is delayed the more difficult becomes the ultimate complete solution.

In these and the many other problems of urban planning and development, there is a challenge and a call to service which must be met. It is for this reason that the Southern Planning Congress that is convening this morning is so important to the South. If it does its work earnestly and well, what it accomplishes may well have profound and continuing effects upon the future of the cities of the South and its people.

CHAPTER III

CITY PLANNING IN THE SOUTH: THE GENERAL PROBLEM

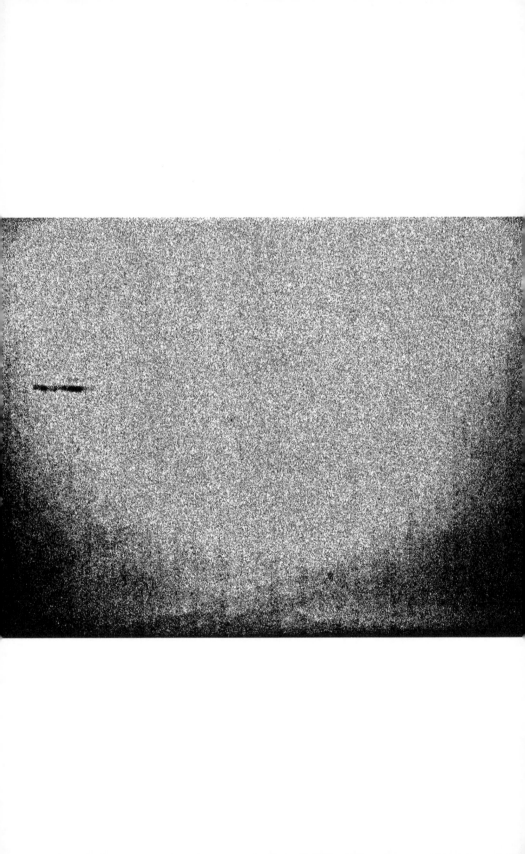

CITY PLANNING IN THE SOUTH: THE GENERAL PROBLEM[*]

* Originally prepared by the Committee on Professional Planning Services for Southern Cities as a part of its final report, the following statement is presented here because it supplies a description of
the general situation faced by city planners in the South in general
and by each Committee of the Southern Regional Congress on City Planning in particular.

he South today is a land in transition from a rural area in which farming was

he most important economic activity to a land of cities and factories. The

hanges which are occurring are affecting the life and social patterns of the

eople of the area to an extent not generally understood. Even a brief examina-

ion of a few basic facts points up the extent of the changes which have occurred

nd suggests the probable future trends. These facts are essential information

o an appraisal of need by local government for professional planning services.

Employment Trends

In the eleven southeastern states[1] in 1929 there were 318 persons engaged in agri-

culture for every 100 persons engaged in manufacturing. By 1952, there were only

105 persons engaged in agriculture for every 100 in manufacturing.

Even though there are still a few more people employed in agriculture in the South

than in manufacturing, income from manufacturing already exceeds income from agri-

culture by a wide margin. For example, in 1929, persons engaged in agriculture

received about 19 per cent of the total income as compared to 15 per cent for

workers in manufacturing. In 1951 manufacturing accounted for 18 per cent of the

total income compared to 13 per cent for agriculture. If these trends continue,

employment in manufacturing as well as income from manufacturing will exceed that

of agriculture within the next decade. Tables I and II show how well defined these

trends have been over the last 20 years.

----

1 Alabama, Arkansas, Florida, Kentucky, Louisiana, Mississippi, North
Carolina, South Carolina, Tennessee, Virginia. The figures would not be sub-
stantially different if compiled for the 14 states represented in the compact
establishing the Southern Regional Education Board.

g	Manu-facturing	Contract Construction	Total Trade & Service	Transp. Com. & Pub. Util.	Trade	Finance	Service	Government
.5	1,320.9	142.8	1,832.8	525.5	778.7	109.1	419.5	488.2
.3	1,202.0	141.2	1,765.7	494.4	750.9	106.6	413.8	495.5
.1	1,026.9	134.3	1,632.5	438.9	698.8	103.0	391.8	506.1
.2	924.0	114.9	1,472.7	381.9	629.8	99.1	361.9	491.0
.1	1,044.5	102.0	1,469.4	364.7	653.2	96.7	354.8	493.1
.3	1,176.4	115.5	1,592.4	378.3	723.0	99.5	391.6	521.3
.6	1,199.2	129.5	1,652.8	385.3	743.3	102.1	422.1	556.3
.4	1,310.3	177.1	1,775.4	413.7	799.6	106.1	436.0	592.8
.5	1,423.3	185.9	1,864.5	438.8	867.3	109.8	448.6	615.1
.8	1,355.4	189.6	1,805.7	402.3	861.9	109.2	432.3	636.8
.1	1,489.4	217.4	1,857.0	417.8	876.3	110.7	452.2	661.4
.1	1,528.8	246.6	1,969.4	440.3	937.9	120.3	470.9	699.8
.8	1,783.0	417.5	2,127.8	474.4	1,019.4	130.0	504.0	783.9
.3	2,038.5	533.2	2,185.5	511.1	1,019.5	127.1	527.8	949.8
.4	2,280.1	387.9	2,261.4	558.8	1,034.1	125.4	543.1	1,096.3
.7	2,273.4	235.0	2,311.4	580.2	1,056.3	130.4	544.5	1,094.8
.6	2,080.8	216.8	2,346.8	579.9	1,084.6	136.1	546.2	1,067.9
.1	2,027.2	277.3	2,577.8	587.8	1,226.4	158.3	605.3	970.1
.8	2,147.9	344.2	2,773.6	605.8	1,341.2	173.0	653.6	940.6
.5	2,179.8	374.8	2,890.3	617.6	1,413.9	186.4	672.4	968.5
.0	2,019.8	362.4	2,878.2	586.2	1,426.4	188.0	677.6	1,015.8
.5	2,141.2	413.4	2,970.6	593.2	1,482.8	203.4	691.2	1,051.0
.5	2,271.4	502.7	3,159.5	630.9	1,580.9	216.2	731.5	1,131.9
.6	2,292.6	531.0	3,268.2	639.9	1,646.8	226.7	755.4	1,192.7

nonagricultural employment, 1939-52, Employment and Payrolls, Annual Supplement, 1953.
ensus reports from BLS estimates for the United States. Persons engaged in agriculture
u of Census estimates for the United States.

Year											
1929	8,142.3	4,203.1	3,939.2	3,451.0	154.5	1,320.9	142.8	1,832.8	525.5	778.7	109.1	419.5
1930	7,906.5	4,158.8	3,747.7	3,252.2	143.3	1,202.0	141.2	1,765.7	494.4	750.9	106.6	413.8
1931	7,599.4	4,173.5	3,425.9	2,929.8	126.1	1,026.9	134.3	1,632.5	438.9	698.8	103.0	391.8
1932	7,268.3	4,158.5	3,109.8	2,618.8	107.2	924.0	114.9	1,472.7	381.9	629.8	99.1	361.9
1933	7,381.1	4,161.2	3,220.1	2,727.0	111.1	1,044.5	102.0	1,469.4	364.7	653.2	96.7	354.8
1934	7,653.4	4,113.5	3,539.9	3,018.6	134.3	1,176.4	115.5	1,592.4	378.3	723.0	99.5	391.6
1935	7,913.4	4,237.0	3,676.4	3,120.1	138.6	1,199.2	129.5	1,652.8	385.3	743.3	102.1	422.1
1936	8,131.0	4,147.0	3,984.0	3,391.2	148.4	1,310.3	177.1	1,755.4	413.7	799.6	106.1	436.0
1937	8,277.4	4,027.1	4,250.3	3,635.2	161.5	1,423.3	185.9	1,864.5	438.8	867.3	109.8	448.6
1938	8,062.6	3,931.3	4,131.3	3,494.5	143.8	1,355.4	189.6	1,805.7	402.3	861.9	109.2	432.3
1939	8,229.8	3,856.5	4,373.3	3,711.9	148.1	1,489.4	217.4	1,857.0	417.8	876.3	110.7	452.2
1940	8,400.0	3,788.3	4,611.7	3,911.9	167.1	1,528.8	246.6	1,969.4	440.3	937.9	120.3	470.9
1941	8,840.5	3,552.5	5,288.0	4,504.4	175.8	1,783.0	417.5	2,127.8	474.4	1,019.4	130.0	504.0
1942	9,406.7	3,510.4	5,896.3	4,946.5	189.3	2,038.5	533.2	2,185.5	511.1	1,019.5	127.1	527.8
1943	9,567.9	3,367.8	6,200.1	5,103.8	174.4	2,280.1	387.9	2,261.4	558.8	1,034.1	125.4	543.1
1944	9,317.3	3,240.0	6,077.3	4,982.5	162.7	2,273.4	235.0	2,311.4	580.2	1,056.3	130.4	544.5
1945	8,896.4	3,030.5	5,865.9	4,798.0	153.6	2,080.8	216.8	2,346.8	579.9	1,084.4	136.1	546.2
1946	8,948.0	3,938.5	6,009.5	5,039.4	157.1	2,027.2	277.3	2,577.8	587.8	1,226.4	158.3	605.3
1947	9,311.0	2,921.9	6,389.1	5,448.5	182.8	2,147.9	344.2	2,773.6	605.8	1,341.2	173.0	653.6
1948	9,423.0	2,820.1	6,602.9	5,634.4	189.5	2,179.8	374.8	2,890.3	617.6	1,433.9	186.4	672.4
1949	9,288.4	2,841.2	6,447.2	5,431.4	171.0	2,019.8	362.4	2,878.2	586.2	1,426.4	188.0	677.6
1950	9,401.4	2,656.7	6,744.7	5,693.7	168.5	2,141.2	413.4	2,970.6	593.2	1,482.8	203.4	691.2
1951	9,728.4	2,496.4	7,232.0	6,100.1	166.5	2,271.4	502.7	3,159.5	630.9	1,580.9	216.2	731.5
1952	9,852.0	2,408.3	7,443.7	6,251.0	158.6	2,292.6	531.0	3,268.8	639.9	1,646.8	226.7	755.4

Sources: Bureau of Labor Statistics estimates estimates of nonagricultural employment, 1939-52; Employment and Payrolls, Annual Supplement estimates for 1929-38 prepared on the basis of various Census reports from BLS estimates for the United States. Persons engaged in agr estimated on the basis of Census reports from BLS-Bureau of Census estimates for the United States.

TVA Division of Regional Studies
Industrial Economic Branch
July 1953
LCC:SS

16

TABLE II

ESTIMATED INCOME PAYMENTS BY MAJOR COMPONENTS: 1929-51

Eleven Southeastern States[a]

Amounts in Millions of Current Dollars

					Trade & Service	Property Income	Govt & Oth Inco
,681	1,670	176	1,325	250	3,459	1,080	726
,136	851	75	759	54	1,970	623	809
,414	1,391	160	1,294	218	3,074	972	1,359
,662	3,267	372	3,867	670	6,976	1,709	5,961
,786	3,710	399	3,873	777	8,342	2,032	4,921
,494	3,969	514	4,500	1,028	8,988	2,182	4,514
,802	4,417	598	4,974	1,231	9,769	2,403	4,629
,141	3,443	495	4,691	1,220	9,807	2,453	5,261
,296	3,531	550	5,447	1,438	10,808	2,789	6,037
,344	4,343	603	6,187	1,890	11,977	2,930	6,779

ma, Arkansas, Florida, Georgia, Kentucky, Louisiana, Mississippi,
lina, South Carolina, Tennessee, Virginia.
stimates of total income do not include payroll deductions for social securit
are not received currently. These deductions are included in the payrolls
his table, since they are not estimated by industry.
sts of net income of farm proprietors, farm wages, and net rents to landlords
farms.
sts of wages and salaries and the withdrawals by proprietors of unincorporated
not include the dividends of corporations.
sts of income from wholesale and retail trade, service, self-employed and
t workers, finance, transportation, communication, and public utilities.
sts of dividends, interest and rents and royalties.
sts of federal civilian and military, state and local school and nonschool
military, veterans' and social security benefits, including a small amount of
dustrial pensions and compensations.

Based on estimates by U.S. Department of Commerce, from special unpublished
igures were added before rounding.

Regional Studies
Economics
1952 LCC:LSS:vs

ion Trends[1]

ft from agriculture to manufacturing as a source of primary employment has
significant changes in work habits and population distribution. In the
s between 1940 and 1950 the total population of the South grew by about
lion. During this period, however, the rural farm population declined by
.4 million. The growth in non-farm population not only made up for the
e of people living on farms but accounted for the increase in total popu-

Viewed in this manner, the total non-farm population grew, during the
from 1940 to 1950, by nearly 10 million people.

of Cities and Towns

portion of the population increase occurred in urban areas which grew
t 7.4 million. The "rurban" population, that is, the people who live in
reas but are not engaged in farming, grew by some 2.2 million.

he South is approaching, if it has not already passed, the point where over
cent of the people are classed as urban. A quarter, although not engaged
ing, live in a rural situation and only a quarter are classed as rural
It is significant that one out of every three people who today live in
n cities did not live there in 1940.

ft from a rural to an urban way of life in the South has lagged behind that
other parts of the nation. To illustrate, as early as 1880, 50 per cent
people in New England were classed as urban. By 1910, 72 per cent of the
land people lived in cities. Since that time the number has increased only
y so that today about 79 per cent live in cities.

_____

The figures in this section apply to the 14 states represented in the
establishing the Southern Regional Education Board.

18

In contrast, in 1880 only 12 per cent of the people in the South were classified as urban. By 1910 this had risen to only 22 per cent. Although there was a steady increase in the number of southern people living in cities and towns, it has not been until the last decade that significant urban growth has occurred.

Guiding the Growth of Southern Cities and Towns

The growth of southern cities presents both problems and opportunities. For the first time many southern cities are faced with problems of housing, traffic congestion, schools, recreation areas, and utilities. City officials are finding no past community experience to guide them in finding solutions. Opportunities result from the fact that most southern cities are in a period of initial growth and are therefore in position to guide community growth so as to avoid the serious problems of urban growth which have been experienced in the older more urbanized sections of the nation.

Cities Are for People

The southern people must grasp the problems of their new environment if they are to adapt themselves successfully to the changes that are taking place. They must understand that cities are the places where over half of the southern people already live. If present trends continue, nearly three quarters of the people of the South may be living in and adjacent to cities in the not too distant future. Look at what happened in New England. It took only 30 years (1880 to 1910) for the urban population of that section of the nation to grow from 50 per cent to 70 per cent.

With the continued industrialization of the South, a similar trend is not unlikely. Yet, unless this process of change is understood and positive steps are taken to guide the growth of cities, there may develop in the South one of the most striking contradictions of our time. Where on the one hand we shall have the results of twentieth century techniques in using and developing natural resources --

the most modern industrial plant as a whole of any section of the country — on
the other hand we shall have a repetition of the outmoded and inefficient cities
which characterize our older urbanized sections of the country with their ap-
parently unsolvable problems of blight, overcrowding, and traffic congestion. If
the hypothesis here advanced is valid and if southern cities and towns become
similar to most of those in northern industrial regions, it will be because the
leaders in southern cities and towns have not seen the opportunities open to them
and have not availed themselves of the known techniques for guiding urban growth.

Planning for Growth

The problem, then, is how can the South guide the development of its cities so
that they will provide healthful and convenient places for an ever-increasing
proportion of its population to live. The magnitude of both the problems and the
opportunities is overwhelming.

The table below shows how cities have grown in both size and number in the past
three decades:

Table III

Size and Number of Cities and Towns
14 Southern States

| Population Group | Number of Cities and Towns | | |
	1950	1940	1930
100,000 or more	30	22	22
50,000 to 100,000	29	25	21
25,000 to 50,000	60	31	34
10,000 to 25,000	199	147	120
2,500 to 10,000	975	710	615
Total	1,293	935	812

Of the total of nearly 1,300 cities and towns in the South, it is estimated that
not more than 200 are undertaking active programs to guide their growth.

20

An active and aggressive planning program designed to meet development problems
as they arise is required in nearly every southern city and town if it is to meet
the challenge of the next 30 years. Too often a city or town waits until problems
become acute or large new industrial developments demand that steps be taken to
plan for future growth. These local planning programs must be devised so that
there will be effective local planning machinery to fit solutions to development
problems, whatever their nature or whenever they occur, into a general plan for
city growth.

In the very largest southern cities such as Dallas, Memphis, Birmingham, New
Orleans, Baltimore, Richmond, and Atlanta the basic development pattern has already been established. Changing these patterns to meet present-day needs will
be a difficult but not impossible task. The great bulk of the southern cities,
as indicated in Table III, have less than 25,000 people. Although some adjust-
ments of the existing patterns may be difficult in the small city or town, the
problems are not nearly as complex as those facing the larger cities. Consequently the smaller city or town has a real opportunity to establish a pattern
for city growth which will meet the needs of present-day urban living.

Intergovernmental Cooperation Necessary

A corporate boundary does not limit city growth. The forces which cause city
growth may result in homes, stores, and factories spreading out over several
jurisdictions. Planning for such basic city needs as streets, schools, recreation
facilities, utilities, and residential neighborhoods requires collaboration between the cities, counties, and other governmental units affected.

On particular problems state and federal agencies may be involved. For example,
the activities of the state in building highways will affect in no small way how
a city or town may develop. Likewise many federal programs affect the development
of cities. State and federal agencies must recognize the need to relate their

plans and programs to those of cities and towns. Unless, however, these local
units of government have effective planning programs, it is difficult to develop
a truly cooperative program for sound and orderly city growth. Federal and state
agencies should conduct their programs in such a way as to encourage the development of sound local planning agencies equipped to carry out their part in a cooperative program.

Even though there are agencies with separate programs at the federal, state, and
local levels, there is no assurance that an effective planning program will result.
Carr and Stermer in their study of Willow Run[1] point out that a major difficulty
in a cooperative program involving several agencies is the absence of an over-all
pattern which defines the roles and lines of cooperation between agencies. They
show, for example, that in the Willow Run situation the federal housing authorities were willing to act in any way possible to relieve the housing conditions.
They could not be effective because there was no machinery by which the agencies
involved could work together. Only when an acceptable and rational pattern for
cooperation is established will it be possible to make effective use of data and
technical assistance which may be available from federal and state agencies.
State planning agencies can take a leading role in developing these relationship
patterns.

Essential Requirements for Local Planning

There are two essential requirements for effective local planning. First of all,
planning must be established as a recognized and continuing function of local
government. Too often the community attitude is expressed by the appointment of
a planning commission which is given the job of preparing a plan for the city or
the county and then is promptly forgotten in the day-to-day decisions which
actually build the city. The work of the commission is not fitted into the

---

1. Carr, Lowell J. and Stermer, James E., Willow Run: A Study of Industrialization and Cultural Inadequacy (New York: Harper, 1952).

administrative machinery of the city. The objectives and policies for building
the city as expressed in the city plan do not have the full support of administrative officials or the citizens of the community. A local planning commission
or planning agency cannot be effective if it works in a vacuum divorced from
other city actions or from the activities of individual citizens.

The second basic requirement for an effective local planning program is that the
planning agency have a continuing source of professional planning advice available
to it. Mr. Dennis O'Harrow, Assistant Director of the American Society of Planning
Officials, in his talk before the Sixth Annual Conference of the Southern Association of State Planning and Development Agencies, stated the need in these terms:
"Planning is a field that can no longer be filled by just any one or even by
busy civic minded citizens with seven other jobs. It is no longer an art of
dilettantes or a function of government that can operate without funds. It is
an art for professionals and is worthy of respectable budget appropriations. It
is important that we take our planning seriously if for no other reason than
because planning our own affairs is the only way we are going to prevent having
our affairs planned for us."

Many local planning agencies fail to function satisfactorily because communities
do not realize that the agency must have technical help if it is to be of any
real service. The problems of city development are so complex that technicians
trained in the methods and procedures for city planning are an essential ingredient
for any effective local planning. In fact, without adequate professional planning
services it is doubtful if the creative job of city building which is so necessary
in the South in the next 30 years can be successfully accomplished.

CHAPTER IV

THE RECOMMENDATIONS OF THE CONGRESS

23

THE RECOMMENDATIONS OF THE CONGRESS

Altogether, 51 recommendations were made by the Southern Regional Congress on City
Planning. Some were specific in their nature; others were general. Many activities recommended were ones which the Regional Committee on City Planning might
undertake under its own auspices; others visualized the Regional Committee as an
agent or catalyst rather than as an enterpriser itself. Taken together, the 51
recommendations covered a large portion of the field of city planning.

The recommendations are presented here not as they were embodied in the Committee
reports at the final session of the Congress, but as they seem to fit together
into three fairly definable groups, regardless of origin.

Research Recommendations

Although one committee was devoted solely to "Basic Research Priorities in
Southern City Planning," several other committees also recommended needed research
projects. A research program of a very wide scope resulted.

Specifically, it was recommended that studies of the following underlying forces
and trends in southern city planning be regarded as "priority research" needs:

1. Population shifts and mobility
2. Major changes in economic patterns and activities
3. Technological and locational patterns of industry
4. New patterns of circulation of people and goods
5. Forces working toward changes in the conditions
   of urban environment
6. Emerging patterns of urban life
7. Natural resources, their use, control and depletion
8. Planning in government
9. Community power structure in urban areas

To the end that work on these high priority research needs of southern city planning might be undertaken immediately, it was further recommended that:

A continuing clearing house committee, widely representative of regional professional organizations and social science disciplines,
be established to serve as a catalytic agent to promote collaboration between agencies and institutions concerned with city planning
in the South on the above and other studies by:

    1. Circulating the above list and any additional information on basic research needs in southern city planning to all such agencies and institutions

    2. Assembling information on research projects contemplated, in process or completed at any of the interested agencies and institutions in the region

    3. Stimulating research among and suggesting research to the said agencies and institutions

and that:

Further work conferences of planners and persons directly involved or interested in city planning be conducted, to the end that a continuous re-examination of planning concepts, premises and approaches may be carried on and that research findings and developing trends in the region may be translated into new and more adequate planning concepts, premises and approaches as required.

While not given a priority label, research of the following kinds was recommended

for early consideration:

    1. Research on sample budgets needed for planning programs in cities of various sizes, the data thus collected to be made available to cities considering planning programs

    2. Research to determine:

        a. What constitutes the most effective and economical pattern of urbanization for the South as a whole and for each of the several states, taking into account the proper servicing of the entire area with urban activities, the proper geographic distribution of economic opportunity, the proper balance of agriculture with other forms of gainful occupation, and the avoidance of conditions tending to invite enemy attack.

        b. What are the upper and lower limits of size for individual cities to insure proper functioning of the local economy and the provision of satisfactory living and working conditions for the citizens.

        c. What developmental pattern for large urban areas is most effective and desirable to insure the optimum combination of sound living and working conditions and reasonable security from enemy attack.

        d. What are the exact nature of and the motivations for current trends in urban expansion in the South and to what extent do they contribute to the objectives suggested as desirable above.

        e. The proper function, land-use pattern and density of aging central areas.

25

3. Research into the following:

    a. Issues and procedures involved in securing interstate cooperation in handling regional planning problems.

    b. Problems resulting from defective governmental structure and the means of solving them.

    c. Means of consolidating at the local level the various types of property controls which are presently scattered through a variety of regulations.

    d. Procedures which are followed in administering planning controls.

4. Research, on the one hand, into the experiences of one hundred corporations of a diversified nature and size which have moved into a broad cross-section of communities throughout the South in the last decade to determine the required community facilities and services for these industries, and on the other hand, into the experiences of the southern communities which have acquired new industries to determine how the planning services of those communities met or failed to meet the needs of incoming industry.

5. Research into the outstanding examples of citizen participation in planning in the South, the results thereof to be utilized as guides for interested parties.

Program Recommendations

A number of the Congress recommendations called for the initiation of specific program activities by the Regional Committee on City Planning. One called for other Regional Congresses on City Planning in the future, at which broader citizen representation might be secured. The others pertained either to educational or editorial activities.

Thus, it was recommended that the following educational activities be undertaken:

1. A program to familiarize such public and private agencies as leagues of municipalities and counties, universities, and industrial and commercial firms working in the developmental field with the contribution they might make toward establishing sound planning practices in their communities, the program to include the development of materials which such agencies might use in providing sound advice and assistance to the organization of local planning.

26

2. A program of civic education in city planning, consisting of:

   a. A workshop for teachers in the elementary and secondary schools in the summer of 1954, to stimulate their interest in promoting civic understanding of city planning in the classroom and to provide them with a foundation for working with a subject so new and different.

   b. The development of a packet of materials designed to introduce elementary and secondary school teachers to the field of city planning and its possibilities as a means of improving the community.

   c. The development of instructional materials and methods to aid elementary and secondary school teachers in promoting understanding of city planning in their classes. Such materials might include an annotated bibliography of planning publications suitable for school use, prepared units of instruction, and listings of resources, persons and agencies.

   d. The preparation of a bibliography of suitable materials, the establishment of working relations with college teachers' organizations, and the consideration of other ways to incorporate the study of city planning in the curriculum at the undergraduate college level in institutions of higher education throughout the region.

   e. The appointment of a committee charged with devising ways and means of strengthening visual aids suited to citizen and school groups, as a vehicle for introducing and motivating civic interest in city planning.

   f. The establishment of better working relations between planning agencies and the press, including radio and television.

3. A tri-partite program in the field of short-course training in city planning, involving:

   a. The conduct of a meeting of representatives of universities, agencies, and organizations interested in sponsoring short-course training in city planning to develop a method by which information on short-course training available in the fourteen-state area may be exchanged and to discuss the problems involved in developing adequate short-courses in city planning.

   b. The establishment of a training center or centers in the fourteen-state area to give two-week courses of supplemental training for members of planning staffs and planning administrators.

   c. The provision of assistance to universities interested in developing short courses of instruction to meet their own needs.

27

4. A program in the field of student recruitment and undergraduate preparation. A permanent coordinating committee on student recruitment and undergraduate preparation, to be composed of at least one representative from each of the states signatory to the Southern Regional Education Compact, should be established to:

   a. Survey, in cooperation with professional planning societies, college course offerings and recommend "pre-planning" programs within the existing curricula.

   b. Secure a centrally administered trust fund for fellowships to be awarded to outstanding applicants to graduate schools of city planning in the region.

   c. Organize a systematic campaign for funds from such sources as philanthropic foundations, civic groups, business and industrial firms, and local, state and national planning agencies interested in obtaining a continuous supply of trained personnel.

   d. Aid and encourage the setting up of undergraduate "on the job training programs" in city planning.

   e. Explore the possibilities in some form of "work-study" program for undergraduates interested in city planning as a career.

   f. Explore the possibilities of schools and other civic groups using other visual materials, such as films and slides, to publicize careers in city planning.

The following editorial activities were recommended:

1. The establishment of an editorial office to carry out three important functions, for the purpose of encouraging planning programs and raising planning standards:

   a. The stimulation and solicitation of articles by southern planners or about southern planning and the channeling of these articles into existing regional, national, and international publications.

   b. The exploration of the possibilities of a planning digest, summarizing articles appearing in non-planning publications but bearing upon the planning field.

   c. The publication of material for planning commission members, other public officials making planning decisions, and community leaders having an impact on planning.

28

2. The development of case materials, to be effected by the establish-
    ment of a committee on case materials and the employment of a
    junior faculty member from one of the universities participating
    in the regional program in city planning to work with the committee in:

    a. Securing the production of case materials by practitioners
        and teachers of planning.

    b. Developing standards and techniques of reporting and
        editing case materials.

    c. Identifying particularly useful case materials early in
        their production and soliciting, if necessary, authors to
        prepare such case studies.

    d. Working out arrangements for the publication and distribu-
        tion of case materials.

3. The rewriting and reproduction of those reports and recommenda-
    tions of the Congress of special interest to business and
    industrial leaders in a suitable form for distribution through-
    out the South.

4. The preparation, publication and distribution to schools, colleges
    and universities throughout the South of an attractive, illustrated
    pamphlet setting forth the prospects and potentials of a career in
    city planning.

eneral Recommendations

large number of Congress recommendations called for action by public bodies

r agencies other than the Regional Committee on City Planning. These recommend-

tions are more in the nature of appeals for action than they are proposals for

articular programs of action. Fifteen such recommendations were made, as follows:

. That all states not now having agencies with broad programs of state planning

d development, including local planning assistance, take the initiative, as a

atter of public policy, to create such agencies.

. That procedures be developed and adopted for assuring careful planning and

ontrol of urban development both within existing corporate limits of cities and

n outside areas that are becoming, or are likely to become, urbanized.

29

3. That pending completion of research, all possible steps be taken to avoid the accentuation of existing urban concentrations that are especially vulnerable to attack and the creation of new concentrations falling in that category.

4. That planners and others concerned with improving the traffic situation, in recognition of the fact that the efficient and speedy movement of people and goods is essential to the over-all prosperity and growth of urban areas,

a. Encourage the use of mass transit, which not only uses street space more efficiently than automobiles, but also requires no downtown parking facilities;

b. Prohibit parking on streets where it interferes with the orderly movement of vehicles, since streets are primarily for the movement of vehicles and people, and not for vehicle storage;

c. Accompany expressways, which are important to the speedy movement of automobiles, trucks and busses, with adequate downtown off-street parking and unloading facilities;

d. Make use of bulk and use zoning controls, combined with off-street parking and unloading facilities, to insure that the demand of the central business district does not exceed the capacity of the transportation routes and vehicles to serve it.

5. That cities develop concrete plans for treating aging central areas, such plans to include:

a. Ways and means of clearing and rebuilding those areas where the land pattern is unadaptable, the structural condition is beyond repair, and/or the land-use is in conflict with current and probable future needs;

b. Ways and means of rehabilitating those areas where the land-use pattern can be changed to meet present and future needs, where the structures are subject to repair, and where continuation of the existing land-use is in accord with the city's master plan;

c. Conservation of structures and neighborhoods in areas where there is evidence of deterioration beginning so that these areas will not sink to conditions requiring more drastic treatment;

d. Low rent housing for those families with income so low that they are forced to live in substandard structures.

30

6. That appropriate steps be taken to correct the critical land-use problem
in the suburban fringes of growing and expanding southern cities, including:

    a. Preparation of a positive plan for residential development,
       implemented by the provision of municipal services and controls;

    b. Development of planned centers for shopping services and places
       of assembly, provided with off-street parking, accessible to
       various modes of transportation, and avoiding conflict with
       major traffic movement;

    c. Planning of adequate land areas properly related to transportation,
       utilities, and labor supply, and protection of these areas for use
       by compatible industries.

7. That planning be coordinated as thoroughly as possible between the official
planning body and the action and operating departments of local government, such
as schools, parks, public works, etc.

8. That capital improvement budgeting be a responsibility of community planning,
and funds not be expended for capital improvements until after receipt of reports
from local planning agencies.

9. That effective mechanisms for planning and land development control on a
metropolitan or regional basis be developed in every such area as quickly as
possible, regardless of political boundaries. Solutions, which cannot be standard
ized for all localities, may include annexation, metropolitan or regional planning
commissions, or the delegation of certain local governmental functions to metropolitan or regional governmental agencies.

10. That a new "model" planning enabling act for local governments in the southern
states be drafted and made available as a guide for new legislation to interested
persons and organizations in each state, and that the following features be kept
in mind in the drafting of this act:

    a. It should be simple.

    b. It should be permissive, rather than mandatory.

c. It should consist of a single, consolidated act, rather than a set of acts.

d. It should include the grant of authority to establish a planning agency and make expenditures for planning; to enact zoning controls (including airport zoning); to regulate subdivisions; to adopt an official map; and to prepare capital expenditures budgets.

e. It should grant such authority to municipalities, counties, and such regional planning agencies as local governmental units may establish by agreements among themselves.

f. It should give local governments discretion as to what type of administrative organization for planning they will use.

g. It should make provision for interim measures to handle emergency situations but should otherwise require that a planning agency be established and that planning activity take place before planning controls become effective.

h. It might include provisions allowing a state agency to exercise temporary controls in particular areas to meet emergency growth situations where local governments have not yet acted.

11. That the formation of statewide planning associations in each state be encouraged, as a means of dissemination of information concerning planning laws, ordinances, court decisions, and effective administrative practices.

12. That the establishment and competent staffing of planning commissions on a municipal, county, and/or regional basis be encouraged.

13. That the planning commission assume the responsibility for the availability of data essential to industry in determining plant location and if necessary stimulate the compilation of such data by the appropriate responsible agencies.

14. That the planning commission recognize, concern itself with and lend encouragement to civic and municipal organizations to establish a program designed to relate and convey to opinion-molding groups the economic values of selective industrial expansion.

32

15. That citizen participation, which is vital and necessary to planning, be
effectuated in at least three points in the planning process:

    a. The citizens of any community should join in determining the
        opportunities for development and needs.

    b. Citizens should assist in the selection of objectives from
        among alternative courses of action.

    c. Citizens should assist in the attainment of the planning
        objectives.

REPORTS OF THE

CONGRESS WORKING COMMITTEES

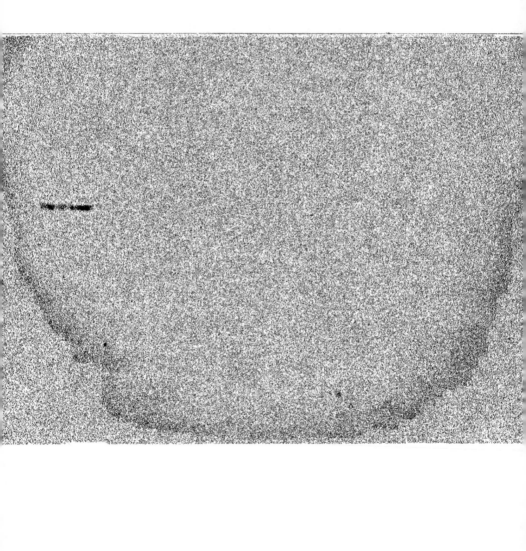

CHAPTER V

PROFESSIONAL PLANNING SERVICES FOR SOUTHERN CITIES

33

COMMITTEE ON PROFESSIONAL PLANNING SERVICES
FOR SOUTHERN CITIES

Committee Members

P. Clayton
stern Office
Bartholomew and Associates
, Georgia

I. Dolbeare
esident - Area Development
a Electric and Power Company
d, Virginia

R. Grand, Head
ent of Architecture and
ing
ity of Florida
ille, Florida

H. Kraft, Chief
n of Local Planning
a Department of Conservation
evelopment
d, Virginia

Donald R. Locke
City Planning Engineer
Norfolk, Virginia

Ernest E. Neal, Director
Rural Life Council
Tuskegee Institute
Tuskegee Institute, Alabama

C. M. Wallace ·
Assistant to the Vice President
Georgia Power Company
Atlanta, Georgia

Joe B. Whitlow
Regional Director
Upper East Tennessee Office
Tennessee State Planning Commission
Johnson City, Tennessee

Aelred J. Gray, Chairman
Chief Community Planner
Tennessee Valley Authority
Knoxville, Tennessee

The Committee on Professional Planning Services for Southern Cities sought an understanding of the nature and extent of professional planning services needed to meet urban development problems in the South and of the possible methods local governments in the region might rely on to obtain the professional planning services determined to be needed.

I

Findings

Cities and counties in the United States and particularly in the South have tried to meet their needs for professional planning services in a variety of ways. A review of some of the methods used may suggest alternatives open to cities and counties concerned with obtaining continuous and adequate technical planning advice.

Local Employment of a Planning Staff

It is generally agreed that the most effective method for obtaining sound technical planning advice is the direct employment of planning staffs by local planning agencies. In cities of over 25,000, budgets may be sufficiently large that this method could be employed successfully. In fact, many of the southern cities of this size already employ their own planning staffs. In the large metropolitan areas staffs of from 10 to 20 people are employed to prepare plans for the orderly development of these areas and to carry out a program which will further orderly and sound development. In some areas there are joint city-county planning agencies employing staffs of from 1 to 6 people. In a few areas professional staffs are employed jointly by two or more planning agencies.

ocedure is difficult because it requires the continued financial and
support of each of the agencies involved.

Consulting Firms

method which has been utilized by many communities has been the employ-
a private consulting firm to assist in the organization of a local
g program and to prepare a comprehensive plan for the orderly develop-
the area. This method has been found to be most effective where there
xisting local planning staff to which the broad experience and know-how
consulting firm can be related. However, many communities having an
Planning commission, but no paid staff, have been able to develop an
ve comprehensive plan in this manner. It has the distinct advantage
ucing a plan within a reasonable time, whereas some communities do a
planning without ever producing a workable guide for their orderly
and continued operation. The consultant and his staff, working closely
e local planning commission and public officials, should reflect, as well
e and direct, the local thinking in the production of the plan.

he plan has been prepared, it may be advisable to retain the consultant
ntinuing basis to assist in its administration. Also, some private
ants have a permanent staff capable of handling the projection of de-
plans for specific areas. This is especially important to the small
ties which are unable to employ capable technicians on a permanent basis.

ssential to recognize that the mere development of a plan will not auto-
ly produce desired results. The plan is but a tool which must be fitted
e whole process of planning which the community should set up to foster
erly development.

e on State Programs of Local Planning Assistance

at bulk of southern cities have less than 25,000 people. In many cases

are not large enough and the amount of work not sufficient to employ a

ne staff. To meet this situation many states have initiated local

g assistance programs. The most outstanding programs of this nature are

South. The Alabama State Planning Board, for example, employs city

s as regular members of its staff. These staff members are available to

and counties throughout the state in preparing studies and plans for

ty and county development. However, Alabama requires that the local gov-

contract for the payment of a portion of the cost of the program.

ar program is under way in Tennessee, where the Tennessee State Planning

ion makes its personnel available to cities and towns in developing their

al planning programs. Both the Tennessee and Alabama programs are unique

ral respects. First of all, these state planning agencies have regional

so that staff members live close to the cities they serve and are able

lop an understanding of both area and city problems. They can and are

le to give technical advice on day-to-day decisions which face municipali-

d which influence the way a particular city or county may develop.

y, the city planners employed by these state planning commissions serve

technical staff for the local planning agency. In this capacity, they

local planning commissions, which are made up largely of lay people, in

ing local planning programs. They undertake broad studies relating to

nomic base, population, and land use, as well as specific studies of

, recreation, traffic, and parking. They prepare for consideration of

nning agency zoning ordinances and subdivision regulations based on the

plan. They assist in the relations between the planning agency and the

partments.

programs are developing in both Virginia and Kentucky. For many years

ginia Division of Planning and Economic Development has had staff members

ourage the formation of local planning agencies. They have not had,

however, sufficient staff to meet the needs for technical services for the many
small Virginia towns. This problem is being discussed and considered by both
official bodies and citizen groups in the State of Virginia. In Kentucky, the
Agricultural and Industrial Development Board initiated a program of local planning assistance in 1951. At the present time only one staff member is employed.
A program is being developed along the lines of the Alabama and Tennessee programs.
Because of limitations of personnel the program during this initial period is
being limited to five or six cities. It is proposed that if funds are available,
the staff providing this service to localities will be expanded within the next
few years.

There is one important aspect of the state programs of local planning assistance
which should not be overlooked. Many of the local planning and development
problems in the South are problems involving several units of local government.
Related to this aspect of the problem is the fact that state development programs in themselves affect local development. It is for this reason that a broad
state planning program is becoming essential for a sound local program. To illustrate, in the northeast section of Tennessee there is a rapidly developing
industrial area made up of a core of four counties with four major cities. Development in any one community affects development in the other communities. Furthermore, some of the industrial plants recently have located in rural areas and draw
their labor force from all communities. It is essential that all of the counties
and communities work together on a common developmental program. At the present
time all of the cities receive technical help from the Tennessee State Planning
Commission, and the assistance of this agency has been the catalyst to further
city-county cooperation on general development plans and programs.

In addition, sound local plans require some understanding of the state program.
For example, it is necessary for the state to work with all of the areas so that

the major street plans of each of the counties and localities can be brought
together into a regional plan which will serve the entire area. The program and
system of state parks will affect each of the local recreation park systems.

It is the belief of the Committee on Professional Planning Services for Southern
Cities that many of the local development problems are actually problems involving several units of local government. For this reason it is becoming increasingly important that the states themselves engage in a state planning program
and stimulate the integration of plans for states, localities and the federal
government.

Other Sources of Technical Planning Assistance

In addition to the activities of state planning agencies, there are other state
institutions which provide some technical assistance. In Florida, North Carolina,
Georgia, Arkansas, and Oklahoma, the state universities have rendered planning
assistance to localities. At the University of Florida, for example, students
have undertaken planning studies of such communities as the Jacksonville Beaches
and Suburbia, and faculty members have served in such communities as Daytona
Beach, Gainesville, and Ocala. The study at the Jacksonville Beaches, undertaken
at the request of the municipal authorities, involved three adjoining communities
along the Atlantic coast where uncontrolled growth, mixed land uses, and contigu-
ous boundaries had created major planning problems. At Suburbia, upon the request of a 100-member citizens' organization, a planning study was undertaken of
a growing gringe area just north of Gainesville. In the space of a few years,
and in accordance with a master plan, Suburbia has secured a new community school,
has acquired ample land adjacent to the school for a neighborhood park, has gotten
a new shopping center under way, has done away with spot zoning for business,
and has completed a number of other worthwhile community projects.

39

Students at Georgia Tech, to list another example, recently undertook a study
of how the city of Cleveland and White County, Georgia, might develop. They
assisted in the drafting of legislation to establish a joint city-county planning
commission which was subsequently appointed. They assisted in the preparation
of. a preliminary master plan including a land-use plan, zoning ordinance, major
street plan and a redesign of the Courthouse Square. Again, in North Carolina
the students, working under the direction of the staff of the Department of City
and Regional Planning of the University of North Carolina, have prepared inven-
tories of. planning needs for many North Carolina cities. These reports have
stimulated the organization of many local planning programs. In some cases staff
members actually give a limited amount of technical advice to local communities.
A similar program is being developed in Arkansas. In 1951 the Institute of Science
and Technology of the University of Arkansas initiated a program of technical and
advisory services through local planning commissions. All work is done by contract.
At the present time the staff is working with five local planning commissions in
cities of from 2,000 to 16,000 population and with housing authorities on plans
for urban redevelopment. The institute works only with official planning bodies
and does not solicit contracts. Services are available to any commission.

Another interesting experiment is being initiated in Florida. For several years
the Florida Improvement Commission has been carrying on a small amount of work
in the field of technical assistance to communities. The 1953 Florida legis-
lature did not provide an appropriation for this activity. As a result, an
effort is being made by the Florida Planning and Zoning Association and the universities to establish at least a source of information within the state on local
planning matters. Although extensive planning assistance will not be available,
it is hoped that establishing a center where information can be obtained, publishing a newsletter on planning progress of Florida towns, and the availability
of a staff member well versed in local planning problems will be of considerable

help to local communities.

In some states, private power and industrial groups encourage and give help in local planning and development matters. For example, the Georgia Power Company for many years has carried on a successful community improvement program. These activities have encouraged community self appraisal which in some instances have led to active official planning programs. As part of this program, the Georgia Power Company furnishes some technical assistance to towns and communities of 20,000 population or less located in its service area. Much of the need for community planning has been evidenced through surveys of possible industrial sites carried on by the private power and industrial groups. These surveys have served to focus attention on the need for planned allocation of desirable sites for industrial purposes if there is to be sound industrial development.

II

Committee Conclusions

Regardless of the source of technical planning assistance, the essential point is that the assistance should be made available in such a way that a continuing and responsible local planning program results. For a state or federal agency or a private consultant to give spot assistance on a particular problem without a going, responsible local planning program is not to recognize the lessons we have learned in the past 20 years. As Roscoe Martin has pointed out, technical assistance is a continuing process which when properly conceived concludes only when the proposal made has been incorporated into the normal practice of the government receiving assistance.[1]

---

1. Roscoe E. Martin, "Technical Assistance: The Problem of Implementation," Public Administration Review, XII (Autumn, 1952), 258-267.

41

Until local governing bodies recognize and support a continuing planning program, only very limited results can be expected from the preparation of comprehensive city plans. The inevitable results are pretty pictures which are occasionally admired and viewed with pride but which have no effect upon the development of the community. The idea of planning as an easy solution to city development problems is an illusion. Unless and until planning becomes an integral part of local government, any over-all general plan cannot be effective.

Professional planning advice is essential to the successful operation of existing programs and those which may be developed in the future. The Committee believes that advice and assistance are needed in three stages of the development of local planning programs:

1. Promotion - When the chamber of commerce or some other local group becomes interested in local planning as a means of developing a better city or county. Information is needed on the general techniques and procedures of planning, on the benefits, and on the costs.

2. Organization - At this stage the community has decided that it may wish to develop a planning program. The city council or county legislative body is interested and wishes to know how to proceed. Some specific help will be needed to prepare local ordinances and in some cases to assist in the preparation of enabling legislation. Technical help will be needed in developing with the chief executive and the governing body the method by which the planning program would be fitted into the present administrative organization of the city or county, what budget will be needed, and how the planning agency would be staffed. This is a technical job and needs careful handling and sound advice.

3. Operation - After the necessary ordinances have been adopted and the local planning agency set up, there is need for continuing, competent staff work to carry the program forward.

The following table has been prepared by the Committee to indicate the existing sources of technical planning assistance available at each stage for each of the 14 southern states. The Committee calls particular attention to sources of technical assistance at the operational stage of a planning program. Believing

42

SOURCES OF TECHNICAL PLANNING ASSISTANCE

PROMOTIONAL STAGE

Source	Ala.	Ark	Fla	Ga	Ky	La	Md	Miss	NC	Okla	SC	Tenn	Tex	Va
State Plan. & Dev.Ag.	X				X	X						X		X
Universities	X	X	X	X		X		X	X	X		X	X	X
League of Municipalities	X				X				X			X		X
ASPO	X	X	X	X	X	X	X	X	X	X	X	X	X	X
Power & Other Ind. Gps.	X	X	X	X	X	X			X	X		X		X
Federal Agencies[1]	X	X	X	X	X	X	X	X	X	X	X	X	X	X
Private Consultants	X	X	X	X	X	X	X	X	X	X	X	X	X	X
City & County Pl.Staffs	X	X	X	X	X	X	X		X	X	X	X	X	X
Citizens Plan. Assn.			X				X							X
Regional Plan. Agencies				X			X							X

ORGANIZATIONAL STAGE[2]

Source	Ala.	Ark	Fla	Ga	Ky	La	Md	Miss	NC	Okla	SC	Tenn	Tex	Va
State Plan & Dev Ag.	X				X	X						X		X
Universities	X	X	X	X				X	X	X			X	
League of Municipalities					X				X					X
ASPO														
Power & other Ind. Gps.														
Federal Agencies[1]	X	X	X	X	X	X	X	X	X	X	X	X	X	X
Private Consultants	X	X	X	X	X	X	X	X	X	X	X	X	X	X
City & County Pl.Staffs	X	X	X	X	X	X	X		X	X	X	X	X	X
Citizens Plan. Assn.			X				X							
Regional Plan. Agencies				X			X							

OPERATIONAL STAGE[2]

Source	Ala.	Ark	Fla	Ga	Ky	La	Md	Miss	NC	Okla	SC	Tenn	Tex	Va
State Plan. & Dev. Ag.	X				X	X						X		X
Universities		X								X				
League of Municipalities														
ASPO														
Power & Other Ind. Gps.														
Federal Agencies														
Private Consultants	X	X	X	X	X	X	X		X	X	X	X	X	X
City & County Pl. Staffs														
Citizens Plan. Assn.			X											
Regional Plan. Agencies				X										

1 In areas affected by certain federal programs and facilities, for example, near national parks, the National Park Service; Tennessee Valley, TVA; Defense areas, HHFA; Savannah River Area, AEC Community Affairs Branch.
2 Competent and trained personnel required at this stage.

the basic need for successful planning programs in terms of technical advice
and assistance is for continuing staff work, the table lists only those sources
of technical help which are available to communities on a continuing basis.
The Committee believes that if this basic need is met there are a great many
sources of technical help for particular aspects of the planning program. These
would include universities, state agencies such as the highway departments, and
federal agencies. Viewing the problem in this manner, the table suggests that
there are, in the South as a whole, a number of sources of technical help available to cities, towns, and counties for the promotion and organization of a
local planning program but that there are only limited sources of technical
assistance available for the operation of the planning program itself.

In meeting this crucial problem the Committee was of the opinion that those cities
with a population in excess of 25,000 could probably finance their own planning
staff. This is the desirable procedure. Wherever possible the city and county
in which the city is located should join together in a single planning program
with a single planning staff. Many of the county problems can only be solved
through collaboration with the city and, conversely, many of the city problems
can only be solved through collaboration with the county. The joint planning
program and staff can help to solve such problems.

The Committee considered that the major problem is the over 1100 small cities
which may not be able to finance a full-time planning staff but in which there
is an urgent need for active planning programs. Many of these towns which are
now small will grow into cities within the next 20 to 30 years. Unless active
planning programs are started now and some way is found by which such communities
will have access to competent technical help, cities in the South will have
missed their greatest opportunity.

44

For this reason there is an urgent need in each of the states for a responsible
agency where at least information on the organization and techniques of local
planning will be available. Wherever possible programs of local planning
assistance should be established in the states. Because of the dynamic nature
of urban growth in the South and the importance of area development as con-
trasted to the development of individual towns, state planning programs are
urgently needed. If states assume this responsibility there could develop in
the South at least a thousand active local planning programs in the next 10
years. This will greatly increase the demand for trained planning personnel.

The Committee suggests that when cities or counties use professional planning
services from whatever source, they be used through a responsible local
planning agency.

The Committee also suggests that cities, in seeking professional planning advice
for the operational phase of their planning programs, recognize that planning
must be a continuing function of local government and that the professional
advice from whatever source should meet two basic needs:

    1. Assistance in the development of basic plans and
       policies to guide city growth

    2. Assistance in the application of these plans and
       policies in day-to-day decision making.

III

Recommendations

Recommendation No. 1

The Committee recommends that the Regional Committee on City Planning propose
to the governors of the 14 southern states through the Southern Regional Education
Board that all states which do not now have agencies with broad programs of state
planning and development including local planning assistance take the initiative

matter of public policy to create such agencies.[1]

ommittee bases this recommendation on the fact that many of the problems of
nization in the South are area planning problems extending over several
dictions. The state is the logical agency to accept this responsibility
rk in the field of area planning, not in the sense of doing the planning
f but in helping to bring together the jurisdictions affected and in pro-
g technical help to the local planning agencies.

such a program the state could take leadership in establishing patterns of
ration between municipal and county governments and between these juris-
ons and the state, thereby filling the vacuum which exists between local
nment and federal agencies.

action in this field is also needed to provide technical assistance and
e to the small southern cities which may not be financially able to sup-
a permanent full-time staff. There are over 1100 cities in the South with
ations between 2500 and 25,000. This is a special problem in the South
se 90 per cent of all its cities are in this category. Furthermore they
sent a third of all cities of this class in the nation.

mendation No. 2

ommittee recommends that a program be initiated by the Regional Committee
ty Planning to develop an understanding of the need for competent advice
ssistance on the part of those public and private agencies whose interests
losely related to urban planning and whose activities make them particularly
to contribute to the advancement of urban planning. Such agencies include
es of municipalities and counties, universities, and private industrial

---

1 The Committee on Citizen Participation in City Planning made an almost
ical recommendation. Since its sense is included in the above recommenda-
it has been omitted from the report of that Committee.

and commercial agencies working in the developmental field.

The Committee makes this recommendation because many of these agencies and groups may not be familiar with the contribution which urban planning makes to the solution of urban problems. Many of them do not realize the contribution which they can make toward establishing planning on a sound basis in southern communities. Many may not be familiar with modern planning techniques and procedures.

To implement this recommendation the Regional Committee on City Planning may wish to develop materials for the use of these groups in providing sound advice on the organization of local planning. The Committee may wish to work with the Southern Association of State Planning and Development Agencies' Committee on Uniform Manuals which has been preparing planning materials for distribution to southern communities.

The Committee might also, as part of its program, request the help of these agencies by a number of means such as direct contact at their annual meetings, invitations to attend the institutes, etc.

Recommendation No. 3
The Committee recommends that research be undertaken or case material collected on sample budgets needed for planning programs in cities of various sizes. The resulting material would be particularly useful to cities considering planning programs.

CHAPTER VI

BASIC RESEARCH PRIORITIES IN SOUTHERN CITY PLANNING

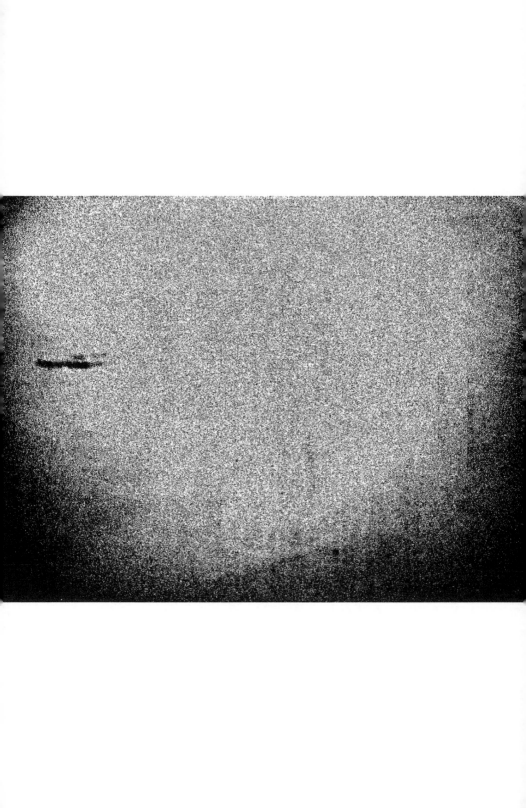

47

COMMITTEE ON BASIC RESEARCH PRIORITIES IN SOUTHERN CITY PLANNING

Committee Members

. Bisso, Director
anning and Zoning Commission
e City of New Orleans
Annex
 Charles Street
eans 12, Louisiana

Carl Feiss, Chief
Planning and Engineering Branch
Division of Slum Clearance and Urban
 Redevelopment
Housing and Home Finance Agency
Washington 25, D. C.

uchanan
ant on Highway Economics
n Regional Education Board
t Peachtree Street, N. W.
, Georgia

H. Kennon Francis
City Planner III
Alabama State Planning Board
102 Church Street
Montgomery 4, Alabama

ullock, Head
ent of Sociology
outhern University
., Texas

Robert B. Highsaw, Director
Bureau of Public Administration
University of Mississippi
University, Mississippi

rt Chapin, Jr.
te Professor
ent of City and Regional
ing
ity of North Carolina
Hill, North Carolina

Dennis O'Harrow
Associate Director
American Society of Planning Officials
1313 East 60th Street
Chicago 37, Illinois

Philip Hammer, Chairman
Executive Officer
Committee of the South
National Planning Association
809 Glenn Building
Atlanta, Georgia

REPORT

Purpose

The Committee on Basic Research Priorities in Southern City Planning was set up
to achieve the following purpose:

> "To attempt to single out and evaluate those urban develop-
> ment problems most urgently needing the spotlight of
> critical analysis".

In the outline of the Committee's purpose drawn up before the Congress, it was
further stated that the Committee would "try to define each problem in terms of
reasonable research possibilities". It was also stated that the Committee
would "set forth means by which a research program for each problem might be
set into motion and the results made known".

In tackling these assignments at the Congress, the Committee recognized that
there would not be time at the meeting to develop suggestions on how a specific
research program might be set up. The Committee felt therefore that it should
spend its limited time probing as deeply as possible into the region's underlying trends and the problems created by these trends and setting forth the
subjects on which basic research for city planning was most urgently needed.

In its two days of joint deliberations, the Committee concentrated upon identifying research needs in terms of the rapidly changing physical and cultural
pattern of the South. The Committee's membership was representative of different
areas and approaches within the region and the discussions were lively and at
the same time geared to fundamental questions.

49

I

Findings

The Committee faced the overwhelmingly important fact that the Southern region
is in the midst of unprecedented changes in its urban living patterns. These
changes are radically affecting the problems which planning is set up to help
solve. They are so fundamental and fast-moving that serious questions are
raised as to the adequacy of traditional planning concepts and approaches to cope
with them.

Within the span of several decades the Southern region has experienced an
urbanization movement comparable to that which took more than a century to come
about elsewhere in the nation. This shift to urban areas has taken place at a
time of unprecedented personal mobility, when the population is literally "on
wheels." The result is that the urban population has been "exploding" into
outlying sections away from the central city and the urban areas are taking on
a brand new look.

The impact of these shifts upon the theory and practice of city planning in the
South is profound. New land-use patterns are developing literally overnight.
Highly complex problems of providing services, guides, and controls are multi-
plying at an astonishing rate. Along with the rapid increase in problems,
there emerges a new promise of unparalleled urban beauty and efficiency. To
keep pace with and overtake the problems and to realize at least a small part
of the promise is the new challenge to city planning in the region.

The basic needs of research are to dig out the facts which are essential for an
understanding of the changes that are taking place and to evaluate their meaning
to planners. Today, research needs may be clearly distinguished from the needs
of twenty or thirty years ago, when planners were virtually "in the dark" about

the problems they faced and when the need was for more light to be thrown upon these problems. Today there is not darkness, but almost too much light - the glare of fast-moving events that blinds planners to their full significance. The ultimate purpose of today's research is to provide an understanding of what is happening so that the tools which the planner is already using to handle his assignments may be realistically reshaped.

Recognizing the fundamental nature of the trends which are taking place in the Southern region, the Committee adopted the following definition of "basic research":

> Basic research is research directed toward an understanding of the underlying forces and trends in urban development and toward the translation of this understanding into planning concepts, premises and approaches.

The Committee recognized that it had to concentrate upon the underlying forces and trends at the Roanoke meeting, rather than upon the planning concepts. It was necessary to take first things first and there was no time to move beyond first things at the meeting. However, the Committee did find time after evaluating the underlying trends to list the major planning concepts that would most likely need re-examination in light of existing patterns and problems.

The Committee's work resulted in a listing of the areas of basic research considered to deserve highest priority for immediate attention. This list is set forth later. The Committee raised and tried to answer the following three questions:

1. Is Southern research for planning likely to develop results of interest and importance primarily to the South or are these results likely to have universal applicability?

2. Should the necessary basic research be done by planners or by members of diverse disciplines, including planning?

3. Should the necessary research be done primarily in the institutions which are parties to the Southern Regional

51

Education Compact, or more broadly by appropriate
institutions generally throughout the region, including the compact schools?

The Committee considered that the first question was more or less irrelevant to
the job at hand. The immediate task was to get an understanding of the underlying forces and trends at work in the region; subsequently, in light of this
understanding, an evaluation could be made of the concepts and approaches em-
braced by southern planners facing day-to-day problems. The Committee felt
that if this subsequent evaluation of the southern planning concepts could hold
definite meaning to areas outside of the South, it would be good; however, no
attempts should be made to consider whether universal applicability did or did
not obtain. The aim of basic research considered at Roanoke should be to help
southern planners better meet southern problems. The task of identifying the
southern situation with the situation of the non-South was left to others who
might later feel an interest in exploring the subject further.

The second question was regarded as extremely relevant. In considering the
underlying trends of the region, the Committee quickly found that the basic
research would have to be done by persons from many different disciplines within
the social sciences. It was clear that the research to be done by planners
themselves would constitute a relatively minor part of the total that was
needed. No real understanding of the different trends is possible without the
analytical and interpretive collaboration of experts from many fields. Research
programs designed to get "answers" most helpful to southern city planners must
recognize this fact and not be limited to the planning field itself or to only
one or two closely related fields.

With respect to the third question, it was also clear to the Committee that no
adequate research program for southern city planning could be undertaken if
limited only to the three institutions which are parties to the Southern

52

Regional Educational Compact. The Committee noted that this was generally
recognized in the following statement included in the proposed cooperative program set forth by the Southern Regional Education Board on October 22, 1952
(and revised in July 1953):

> "A jointly conducted research program can utilize the par-
> ticular facilities and competencies of each of the three
> institutions, and enlist the aid of collaborating agencies
> and institutions."

Although this statement does recognize the necessity of enlisting the aid of
"collaborating agencies and institutions," the Committee felt that the statement in itself was too limited in its scope and might be re-phrased to emphasize
the absolute necessity of inter-institutional collaboration on a much wider
basis than within the framework of the Compact itself. Instead of "enlisting"
the aid of other organizations, a competent research program would literally
have to be built upon their cooperation. The recognition of this fact implies
also recognition of the tremendous scope of the research program that is needed
and the necessity of preserving the interdependence of the various disciplines
and of the various institutions and agencies involved.

II

Committee Conclusions

Research priorities

As already indicated, the Committee believes that the highest immediate priority
should be given to research projects aimed at an understanding of underlying
trends and forces rather than at planning concepts and techniques. It recognizes that the latter type of research must be undertaken as soon as possible,
but can be undertaken only in light of the results of the research in trends
and forces.

53

Below are listed the areas of basic research in forces and trends which the
Committee considered deserving of the highest priority for immediate attention.

Of high immediate priority:

    1. Studies of Population Shifts and Mobility

        The "revolution" that is taking place in the physical
pattern of the South is only beginning to be understood,
not only by planners but also by other groups affected
by the basic shifts which are underway. The rural-urban
and urban-suburban movements within the region are caus-
ing a situation of intense fluidity. Major problems which
haunted city planners in other areas two or three decades
ago are being virtually by-passed in the South (for example,
the extremely high densities of central cities). The new
patterns of physical land use and culture must be clearly
understood if the problems are to be met and the potentialities realized. Studies need to be made of the:

        a. Shifting patterns of population distribution
           (rural to urban, central city to suburban,
           etc.).

        b. Changing population composition in urban areas
           (age, sex and race).

        c. Increased family mobility (within and between
           cities and areas).

    2. Studies of Major Changes in Economic Patterns and Activities

        The South is also undergoing an "economic revolution" in
addition to the profound changes in population (of course,
the two trends are integral parts of same basic forces).
New plants are moving to the region and new industries are
springing up to utilize both natural and human resources
that are at hand. Both the out-migration and the internal
shift of population, coupled with increased economic activity,
are resulting in higher income per capita and per family.
The occupational patterns of income distribution are getting
closer to the national averages. Studies are already underway on some of the problems (the work of the Southeastern
Economic Research Conference is a case in point) but a great
deal of work needs to be done. Further studies should be
made of the:

        a. Shifting sources of individual income.

        b. Major geographical patterns of income payments.

        c. Changing distribution of population by occupational
           groups.

      d. Shifting structure of public finance (revenue
         base and yield, expenditures and debts, re-
         lations of federal, state and local tax systems).

3. Studies of Technological and Locational Patterns of Industry

Thousands of new industrial plants are being located throughout
the region and their location is a major factor in physical
planning. In some instances, the location marks the beginning
of new towns and communities. In other instances, the location
is primarily significant because of its relation to existing
near-by land-uses. Technological developments in plant design
have made possible new locational patterns which the South is
in a position to take advantage of during its period of
growth. Study should be made of the:

      a. Shifting patterns in the location of new
         industrial sites.

      b. Characteristics of new industrial operations
         (physical and labor patterns, creation and
         control of nuisances, etc.).

      c. Relation to new industrial locations and
         community resources.

      d. Factors of attraction and interdependence
         of industrial plants.

      e. Industrial location and defense dispersal.

4. Analysis of New Patterns of Circulation of People and Goods

Circulation becomes the major problem in the region's new
urban areas which are spreading out so rapidly in all di-
rections. It is already obvious that Southern cities and
metropolitan areas cannot accommodate effectively the
increase in motor vehicular traffic wishing to utilize
street surfaces and parking space. These areas face complete traffic stagnation and a denial of the great promise of
the future unless problems of circulation can be solved.
They might be solved by studies of the:

      a. Optimum transportation systems and methods in
         expanding urban centers.

      b. Desire patterns of urban traffic generation
         and direction.

      c. Relation of traffic financing, land values
         and taxation.

      d. Shifts in technological patterns of air, rail,
         and truck circulation.

55

5. Studies of Forces Working Toward Changes in the Condition
   of Urban Environment

Although southern cities have avoided many of the major
problems of over-concentration in the central city, basic
forces are at work and are progressively blighting both
property and neighborhood values. The outward dispersal
of population, while decreasing blight in some areas,
increases the spread of blight in others. The fluidity in
new land-use development itself can result in bad as well
as good patterns. In some ways, southern cities are making
the same mistakes that cities elsewhere made a half century
ago but with less reason. Research needs to be done on the:

   a. Differences in the condition of the physical
      structure of parts of urban communities.

   b. Effects of industrialization, circulation,
      dispersal, population mobility, and commercial
      decentralization upon blight, slums, and deter-
      ioration of property and community.

   c. Effects of blight on people, government costs,
      and social development.

6. Studies of Emerging New Patterns of Urban Life

The pressures of urbanization in the South are creating a
variety of changes in the attitudes and habits of city
people - as individuals, families, and groups. The individual has a host of "desire patterns", both hidden and
apparent, needing identification. There are a variety of
"habit patterns", developed around the daily, weekly and
seasonal needs of the family (for example, neighboring,
shopping, and recreation). There are also distinct "action
patterns" of informal and formal groups in the community
calling for recognition. More needs to be known about
these changing patterns and the relation between them and
physical land-use patterns in the future. In particular,
the following need to be known: the

   a. Trends in family habits and desire patterns
      calling for adaptation of planning methods
      and programs.

   b. Changes in physical land-use patterns (new
      design patterns and new locational relations
      of land uses).

Of lesser priority but urgently needed

   1. Studies of Natural Resources and their Use, Control and Depletion

   The totality of resources constitutes a vital part of the
   economic fabric of the South. Either directly or indirectly

the total resources available to an area are involved at
each stage of its development. Effective planning must
provide for the efficient use of all resources and for the
balanced development of resources on an area rather than
an individual municipal basis. Research has already gone
forward in this field by state and local agencies and by
the Southeastern Public Administration Council. It needs
to tackle now the:

    a. Location and description of renewable and non-
       renewable reserves of land, forests, minerals,
       water, and other resources.

    b. Administrative patterns to promote the balanced
       development of physical resources on an area
       basis.

    c. Administrative patterns to safeguard and control
       resources within the region.

2. Studies of Planning in Government

Although the mechanisms and techniques of planning fall
within the scope of "applied" research rather than "basic"
research, there are underlying trends in the development
of the planning function that need study as a part of a
"basic research" approach. Population and economic shifts
are reflected in attitudes (both inside and outside of
local government) which in turn create a favorable or un-
favorable climate in which planning can function. Similarly,
these basic trends have sparked the development of new
governmental patterns into which planning must be organi-
zationally tied. The following research problems in
particular need attention:

    a. Trends in the organization of planning in
       local government.

    b. Patterns of administration for carrying out
       planning within local government.

    c. Inter-government problems resulting from
       differences between local areas of "geographical
       unity" and local areas of "political unity".

3. Studies of Community Power Structure in Urban Areas

The success or failure of planning is often determined
by the attitude of the "invisible government," which is
made up of democratic leadership groups within the community which determine the conditions under which action
programs are accepted and go forward. Within the South,
there has always been a predominantly "rural" flavor to

the urban leadership and a homogeneity of urban population that has been distinctly different from the
heterogeneity of cities in the non-South. The recent
increased shift in population from rural to urban areas
has increased the pattern of "rural" leadership in the
South's urban centers. The implications of this phenomenon
are of profound importance to city planning and much more
needs to be known about it. Work needs to be done on the:

a. Identification of psychological patterns in the
   community that affect planning.

b. Identification of new and changing patterns of
   urban leadership control.

c. Identification of special interest groups in
   the planning process.

Planning concepts

There are a number of planning concepts which have formed the framework in which

planners have undertaken their work. Many of these concepts were developed

during the '20's and '30's when the conditions and circumstances were vastly

different from those of today. It is also true that most of the basic con-

cepts which govern the thinking and action of planners were developed in terms

of city problems in the non-South.

The Committee strongly suspects that a re-evaluation of these concepts as they

have significance to the southern planner today might show that many are un-

realistic and ill-adapted to the situation faced by planners in the region.

However, these concepts cannot be re-evaluated except in terms of an understand-

ing of the underlying trends which have brought about conditions sharply differ-

ent from those in which the concepts were originally born. Consequently, the

Committee recognizes that basic research in the field of planning concepts must

await completion of at least some of the analysis and interpretation of under-

lying trends that have already been proposed.

Some question might be raised as to whether research in planning concepts is

"basic" in the same sense as research in underlying forces and trends is "basic".

58

It will be recalled that the Committee's definition of "basic research" included
the "translation of this understanding /of underlying forces and trends/ into
planning concepts, premises and approaches." The Committee made a sharp dis-
tinction between "basic" as defined in this way and "applied" research, which
might be posed as the other main approach that can be made. "Applied research"
is taken to cover research in the techniques and mechanisms of planning -- the
"how" and "when" rather than the "why" and "what". The Committee felt that its
assignment at the Congress definitely did not include an evaluation of the "how"
and "when" techniques.

The Committee felt that it might be helpful to list a number of the most commonly
held planning concepts, a subsequent analysis of which is badly needed as part
of the basic research program. Among the concepts particularly suggested for
re-evaluation, either immediately or upon the completion of the pertinent basic
research in underlying forces and trends, are the following:

1. Optimum size city.

2. Optimum population density.

3. The neighborhood unit (immediate research into
   model towns that are already in existence).

4. Optimum land-use patterns.

5. Optimum distribution of land for different purposes.

6. Standard methods of land-use guides and control
   (zoning, subdivision control, and master plan).

7. Autonomous departmental organizations in local
   government for planning, development, and control
   (building department, inspection department, zoning
   department, etc.).

8. Metropolitanism

9. Limitation of land-use in the name of efficiency.

10. Right to the free use of public streets and rights-of-way.

11. Assumed permanence of existing social institutions.

12. Standardization in housing.

59

III

Recommendations

As already indicated, the Committee feels that drastic changes are taking place in the physical pattern of the South. It feels that it has been able only to scratch the surface of this subject during the Roanoke Congress. A great deal of thinking must be done, even in the preliminary identification of the areas in which basic research is most needed.

In general, therefore, the Committee's recommendations are not "final" ones in the sense that any substantive conclusions were reached at the Congress. What is indicated is immediate follow-up action to make certain that the research facilities in the region are mobilized as rapidly as possible to undertake the jobs which are ahead.

The Committee's specific recommendations to the Congress are as follows:

Recommendation No. 1

That the Congress approve the transmittal of the above list of studies in underlying forces and trends to the Regional Committee on City Planning for use as described below.

Recommendation No. 2

That the Congress recommend to the Regional Committee on City Planning that it establish a continuing clearinghouse committee widely representative of regional professional organizations and disciplines whose functions would be:

      a. to circulate information on basic research needs in southern city planning to all concerned agencies and institutions throughout the region, beginning with the list of projects set forth above and to which further   priorities and items might be added;

b. to assemble information on research projects completed, in process, or contemplated in said institutions and helping to meet the city planning research needs set forth above; and

c. as a general purpose to stimulate among institutions and agencies within the region continuous research projects needed for city planning.

Resolution No. 3

That the Congress recommend to the Regional Committee on City Planning that it conduct further work conferences of planners and persons directly involved in or interested in planning: (a) to carry on a continuous re-examination of planning concepts, premises and approaches; and (b) to translate additional research findings and underlying trends in the region into new and more adequate planning concepts, premises and approaches, as required.

Footnote on Recommendations

With respect to the recommendations that a continuing clearinghouse committee be established by the Regional Committee on City Planning, it might be noted that the recommendation is that the membership of this committee should be broadly representative of "regional professional organizations and disciplines." It is important to avoid a representation based upon institutions and agencies, so far as possible, and to rely more upon professional organizations and disciplines. Institutional representation can easily result in difficulties arising from the autonomous nature of the institutions involved. It is almost impossible to get representation on the "vertical" basis without slighting one or more institutions. On the other hand, the use of the "horizontal" professional organizations guarantees a reasonably adequate representation of institutions and obviates any feelings on the part of specific institutions that they might have been overlooked.

61

The Committee would also like to emphasize again the importance of collaboration of all the disciplines in the social sciences in the basic research needed for southern city planning. The sooner the different disciplines are brought into consideration of planning problems on the research level, the better it will be for the disciplines and planning research itself. It is significant that a great part of the basic research proposed by this Committee will obviously have to be undertaken by persons other than planners themselves.

The Committee would also like to suggest that the clearinghouse committee which might be set up by the Regional Committee on City Planning be given only a catalytic function. There are any number of excellent research programs already under way in the South which have an autonomy of their own. The new clearing-house committee should in no way interpose itself between these existing research programs and possible sources of funds, nor should it be put in a position of trying to direct the nature of the autonomous research programs or the emphasis of their work. At the same time, the clearinghouse committee can be in a position to promote in a positive way an even greater collaboration among the various agencies and to suggest the areas most needing additional attention.

The Committee does not believe that there would necessarily be any direct connection between the clearinghouse committee and the further work conferences of planners which it is proposed the Regional Committee on City Planning might undertake in the future. The clearinghouse committee is to be a catalytic agency broadly representative of various social science disciplines in the region. On the other hand, the work conferences of planners would be more concerned with the problems of the planning research itself. At the same time, it is recognized that the results of the clearinghouse committee in promoting basic research will have a direct bearing upon the effectiveness of the work conference.

CHAPTER VII

CIVIC EDUCATION IN CITY PLANNING

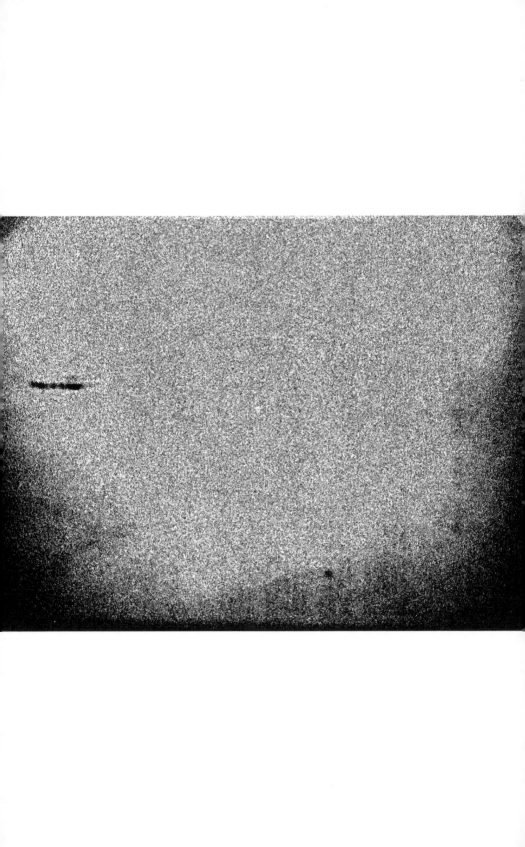

62

COMMITTEE ON CIVIC EDUCATION IN CITY PLANNING

Committee Members

Brown, Assistant Director
unty Research Foundation
tropolitan Building
Second Avenue
Florida

Harlean James, Executive Secretary
American Planning and Civic Association
901 Union Trust Building
Washington 5, D. C.

Creese
. Hite Art Museum
ity of Louisville
lle 8, Kentucky

Helen F. Kyle
Assistant Professor of Education
College of Education
University of Oklahoma
Norman, Oklahoma

W. Dibble
W. Dibble and Company
ants
h Main Street
South Carolina

Milo M. Smith, Director
Cobb County Planning Commission
City Hall
Marietta, Georgia

lora, Chairman
a City Planning Commission
good Avenue
a, South Carolina

John Elliott Wood
Town Planning Consultant
423 West Main Street
Elizabeth City, North Carolina

Margaret Carroll, Chairman
Planner
Harland Bartholomew and Associates
Atlanta, Georgia

63

REPORT

Purpose

The purpose of the Committee on Civic Education in City Planning was to reach
agreement on the nature of the problems involved in its field of interest and
to formulate ·a positive program of action, with recommended means of accomplishment, for the progressive improvement of civic education in city planning.

I

Findings

City planning has always been faced with a lack of understanding and active
interest on the part of citizens. Documentation is hardly needed to demonstrate
that the majority of them are completely unaware of its function as a means of
improving community living. Now, however, when the communities of the South are
changing so rapidly, there is a new urgency for civic education in city
planning. As the rate of urbanization has accelerated, so has the complexity
of municipal and urban problems. Suburbs grow untended, and rural communities
face new calls for facilities and services that hitherto were regarded as
the amenities of city life. If the growing number of problems attendant upon
urbanization are to be met in a satisfactory manner, the self governing ·people
of the cities and their suburban fringes must become aware of city planning as
a function of government and as a means to better living, so that their support
and understanding can be relied on.

II

Committee Conclusions

The Committee on Civic Education in City Planning concluded that four groups
present the best opportunities and bear the greatest responsibility for carrying

out civic education programs in city planning. Those groups are:

1. official bodies, such as planning commissions, boards of zoning adjustment, etc.

2. educational institutions at all levels

3. civic groups, clubs and youth organizations

4. professional planners

Such official bodies as planning commissions and boards of zoning adjustment can provide leadership in civic education in city planning by:

1. seeking the cooperation of the communications agencies in the community in the timely publicizing of particular planning events, new phases of the planning program, and announcements of general interest concerning its implementation.

2. inviting representatives of various civic groups to attend board sessions to become better acquainted with the planning program in general (many civic groups have "Civic Affairs" or "City Planning" Committees). Representatives of specific groups might be invited when a topic in which they have manifested an interest is under discussion.

3. making contact with professional societies in the community. Since members of planning commissions, etc., are likely to be members of one or more of these societies, this should be quite easy to accomplish. It will present a potent opportunity for educating a high echelon of leadership in the community.

4. calling on members of professional societies for aid in solving specific problems; e.g., lawyers re planning legislation, engineers re major thoroughfares, realtors re zoning, and health and welfare people re substandard housing. Enlisting their help should arouse their interest in the planning program and thus prepare the ground for their activity in civic education.

5. holding effective public hearings. If the members of a planning commission or board of zoning adjustment are thoroughly informed on the issues at hand, and are thus able to help the planning technicians carry the ball, public hearings may be made educational experiences. The feasibility of holding public hearings on important programs, such as zoning, on a neighborhood basis, should be investigated, if the size of the city permits such decentralization.

6. sponsoring publication of popularized pamphlet summaries of lengthy technical reports for wide local distribution. A series of single sheet throw-aways on various phases of the planning program might be undertaken also.

65

The field of public education affords many opportunities for promoting civic understanding of city planning. The findings of the 1948 and 1951 surveys of the activities of planning agencies in connection with the public schools were reviewed. Preparation of a questionnaire designed to bring these surveys up to date was discussed. It was agreed that a bibliography of planning publications suitable for school use should be prepared and given wide distribution. The following propositions as to the place of city planning in the curriculum were studied:

1. City planning instruction as a suitable phase of existing school subject patterns.

2. City planning instruction as it might serve as a foundation for a core curriculum around which many subjects are grouped.

3. City planning instruction as a means of teaching citizenship and community living.

The Committee recognizes that there are a number of problems involved in carrying out civic education in city planning through educational institutions. There is an acute need for workshops on city planning to give teachers a foundation for working with a subject so new and different. There is a pronounced scarcity of suitable materials. A way must be found of making information from technical reports on local planning programs usable for classroom purposes. There are difficulties to be overcome in getting students out of the classroom and into the community. The aid and interest of local officials and resource people must be enlisted. It is hard to lead students to learn for themselves by studying their community. Situations must be created in which students and teachers may learn together. Since the best kind of community study cannot be given in textbook capsules, this situation calls for additional teaching skill.

Civic groups, clubs and youth organizations whose area of interest and purpose relate to city planning also have a role to play in civic education in city planning. They might be encouraged to invite qualified persons to fill the role of guest speaker. Suburban and rural groups with such pressing problems as

roadside beautification, zoning and fringe area development might be especially
amenable to such speakers. The Committee recognizes the difficulty of making
technical material understandable to a non-technical audience and suggests the
use of films, slides, maps, charts, etc., as one way around it.

The professional planner himself is all important in developing a civic education program. Much of the responsibility for leadership will be his. He
is in the best position to know what publications, films, exhibits, and the
like are available. He is best acquainted with data on local planning problems.
He will be likely to know about successful civic education activities elsewhere
in the nation. The planner can be the idea man, stimulating others to act. His
participation is essential.

The Committee believes that each of the following media can be appropriately
used by the above groups in carrying out a civic education program:

1. Press.

   It is particularly important to develop a continuing working
   relationship with the press. Many phases of a planning program are good copy, especially if care is taken to provide
   illustrative material to accompany the news story. Properly
   timed, news releases can be very helpful. There is considerable value to a Sunday feature or magazine supplement type
   article on the overall planning program in a community.

2. Radio and Television.

   Although there is a problem in finding or adapting visual
   materials for use on television, radio and television programs are of demonstrable value in giving a community general
   information about civic affairs and specific material on
   current planning issues. Programs utilizing city officials,
   commission members, members of civic groups, school students,
   etc., whether the panel or the interview type, offer promise
   to a civic education program in city planning.

3. Films,

   Films are an excellent means of reaching the public. The
   Committee voiced the need for a film on city planning,
   suitable for the southern region. It would be desirable
   for such a film to explain city planning and to give examples
   of good planning and the lack of it. It should be designed
   to lend itself to follow-up with specific material on

particular local planning programs. Such a film could be
used by civic groups, school and college groups, television
producers, at public hearings, etc. An exploration should
be made of ways in which such a film could be planned, pro-
duced and financed.

4. Other.

The possibilities for developing exhibits, slides, film
strips and publications suitable for regional distribution
should be considered at some future session. The Committee
was not able to devote sufficient time to the study of these
media of education.

III

Recommendations

After considering the areas for action in a civic education program in city
planning, the Committee on Civic Education reached the decision that the most
important area for immediate consideration was the development of materials and
methods for working with the schools. The area of instruction presenting the
most promising immediate possibilities appeared to be kindergarten through
twelfth grade. The first three recommendations are directed to this end.

Recommendation No. 1

That the Regional Committee on City Planning consider the sponsorship of a workshop for teachers to be held in the summer of 1954. The purpose of this workshop
is to provide stimulation and articulation between professional planners and
teachers, leading to a common basis on which materials and methods might be
evolved.

Recommendation No. 2

That the Regional Committee on City Planning consider the development of such
instructional materials as an annotated bibliography, prepared units of instruction, and listings of resources, persons and agencies to assist teachers in bring-
ing planning into the curriculum. The development of these materials should lay

stress on quality rather than on quantity. All listings should be thoroughly
annotated as to their suitability in terms of subject matter fields, level of
education and the type of community to which the materials would be applicable.

Recommendation No. 3

That the Regional Committee on City Planning consider the preparation and/or
selection of a packet of materials for the use of teachers, designed to introduce them to the field of planning and to its possibilities as a means of improving the community. This should provide a stimulus to the imaginative and
enterprising teacher to incorporate this means of community improvement as a
part of his instructional program.

The above recommendations reflect the present need for a working relationship
between school and planning programs when both profess the same goal of community
improvement; the dearth of usable materials, which have been judged by accepted
criteria of age level, subject fields, and adaptability to the southern region;
and the unusual problems encountered in the teaching of community planning and
the special skills required. Ways of implementing these first three recommendations are numerous. The Committee decided that the principle of working through
already established agencies, institutions, and programs, such as state departments and colleges of education, pre-school workshops, and post-school planning
conferences, committees of national and state education associations, etc.,
should be observed in selecting courses of action.

Recommendation No. 4

That visual aids, suited to citizen and school groups, be strengthened, thereby
serving to introduce and motivate interest in the field of city planning. The
lack of audio-visual aids suited to the size and nature of communities that
characterize this region, and the lack of materials treating the special problems
of southern communities, such as recent trends in growth and industrialization,
account for this recommendation. The Committee proposes that this recommendation

emented by the establishment of a regional committee charged with the

f the subject matter, resources for production, and financing of such

isual aids.

ndation No. 5

e Regional Committee on City Planning study the development of methods foi

rating the study of city planning as a part of the curriculum at the under

e level of instruction in institutions of higher education throughout the

Since a large segment of our civic leadership comes from the college

citizens of southern communities, it is important that a teaching pro-

developed at this level, separate and distinct from the undergraduate

g of the professional planner. This recommendation might be implemented

development of a bibliography of materials suitable for instruction at

vel, including materials on planning in general and materials designed to

planning to specific subject matter fields such as history, geography,

gy, and fine arts. Working relations with college teachers' organizations.

the American Studies Group, the geographers, the urban sociologists,

lso be established.

ndation No. 6

e Regional Committee on City Planning give further study to ways of util-

he principal media for public information -- press, radio, and television -

ic education. The Committee feels that there is need for more technical

nce to planners on the use of these channels of communication, since they

mendously important as means of information, formulation of opinion, and

s to action. The Committee recommends that the Regional Committee on

anning study means of establishing better working relationships between

g agencies and press, radio and television agencies.

CHAPTER VIII

A PLANNING PERIODICAL

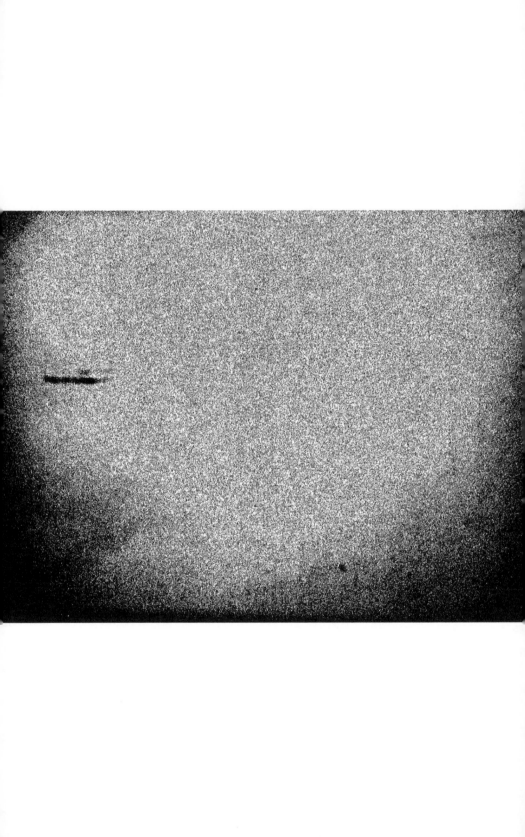

70

COMMITTEE ON A PLANNING PERIODICAL

Committee Members

Mozell C. Hill, Chairman
Department of Sociology
Atlanta University
223 Chestnut Street, S.W.
Atlanta, Georgia

Dudley Hinds, Regional Director
West Tennessee Office
Tennessee State Planning Commission
Jackson, Tennessee

Henry L. Kamphoefner, Dean
School of Design
North Carolina State College
Raleigh, North Carolina

Raymond V. Long
Commissioner and Acting Director
Department of Conservation and
  Development
Richmond, Virginia

Reed Sarratt
Editorial Director
JOURNAL and SENTINEL
Winston-Salem, North Carolina

Barbara Terrett
Planning and Housing Officer
District of Columbia
  Redevelopment Land Agency
499 Pennsylvania Avenue, N. W.
Washington 4, D. C.

Mary Ellen Ward
Box 177
Avon Park, Florida

Albert Lepawsky, Chairman
Professor
Department of Political Science
University of Alabama
University, Alabama

Purpose

The core concern of the Committee on a Planning Periodical was to find ways of improving the communication of planning ideas and experiences, through the medium of publications, among: (1) professional planners, including planning commission staff members, related technicians working for agencies having planning responsibilities, and planning educators; (2) members of planning commissions; (3) governmental officials responsible for applying plans or planning decisions, including mayors and other local executives, municipal councils and other local legislatures, and administrators of major governmental services and departments; and (4) community leaders having an impact upon planning decisions. The Committee on a Planning Periodical did not concern itself with planning publications directed toward the general public.

I

Findings

A Committee questionnaire answered by half the Congress delegates elicited the following facts: of sixty-three professional and semi-professional periodicals listed by the delegates, those most frequently read or regularly consulted were the Journal of the American Institute of Planners, the News Letter of the American Society of Planning Officials, the American City Magazine, the Town Planning Review (British), Planning and Civic Comment, Land Economics, Architectural Forum, Landscape Architecture, the Community Planning Review and the Journal of Housing. Other publications read ranged from the broadly-based social science publications to the technical publications in fields related to planning.

question of whether a new planning periodical is desirable, about fifty
t of the respondents felt it was, twenty-five per cent were flatly op-
o the idea, and twenty-five per cent were undecided. The reasons listed
e opposed ranged from the feeling that existing journals should be
hened by contributions from the South to the danger that a southern
 might have a parochial character. Those favoring a new periodical were
eans agreed upon its character or its form.

mittee also consulted the editors of fifteen planning journals in the
States and abroad. Ten editors replied, and five provided considerably
d information for the Committee's purpose. These editors represent
s mainly directed toward and subscribed to by members of professional
ations in whose names the journals are published. Most of the editors
d the precarious financial base of their publications and they emphasized
essity of obtaining a subsidy of one kind or another. In the case of
n Planning Review, for example, the publishers are now conducting a
n in this country for financial contributions that would permit the
 to continue publication during the ensuing year.

the most interesting and frequent comments in the responses of the editors
the effect that practically no fresh planning material is contributed to
ournals from the South. At the same time, the editors warned the
ee about the difficulty, and possibly the unlikelihood, of securing
publishable material to justify a new planning periodical.

 regional periodicals have been proposed recently for the South. One,
s Letter of the Southeast Chapter, American Institute of Planners, is
d primarily for the southern members of this organization. The other,
icipal South, which the Clark-Smith Publishing Company is contemplating,
al with municipal government in general, but will possibly give substan-
tention to planning news.

73

II

Committee Conclusions

The Committee on a Planning Periodical does not believe the evidence justifies
the establishment of a new planning periodical in the South. It does not feel,
however, that existing publications in and out of the planning field meet all
the requirements of persons concerned with planning in the region. Even the
two regional periodicals recently proposed do not offer that promise.

III

Recommendations

On the basis of the data presented above and after further deliberation, the
Committee recommends that an editorial office be established by the Regional
Committee on City Planning to carry out the following functions:

1. To stimulate and solicit articles by southern planners
   or about southern planning and to channel these articles
   into existing regional, national and international
   publications, both professional and popular.

2. To explore the possibilities of a planning digest summarizing articles appearing in publications not read generally
   by planners but bearing upon the planning field.

3. To publish material for planning commission members, other
   public officials making planning decisions, and community
   leaders having an impact upon planning, with the object of
   stimulating planning programs and raising planning standards.
   The exact content, format and frequency of such publication
   or periodical should be determined after further study and
   experience by the editorial office.

CHAPTER IX

CITY PLANNING PROBLEMS OF THE CENTRAL
CITY AND SUBURBAN FRINGE

74

TTEE ON CITY PLANNING PROBLEMS OF THE CENTRAL CITY AND SUBURBAN FRINGE

Committee Members

. Augur
llnerability Specialist
of Defense Mobilization
ve Office of the President
ton 25, D. C.

Davis, Vice President
a Transit Company
th Davis Avenue
d 20, Virginia

W. Hawkins
r of Development
le Housing Authority
th Sixth Street
le 6, Tennessee

James, Director
on Division
ive Safety Foundation
g Building
ton 6, D. C.

awson, Manager
ty and Rural Development
tment
arolina Electric and Gas
ny
a, South Carolina

Edmund W. Meisenhelder, III
Consultant on Municipal Management
Municipal Technical Advisory Service
Nashville, Tennessee

George R. Pappas, Project Officer
Human Resources Research Institute
Air University
United States Air Force
Maxwell Air Force Base, Alabama

Herbert F. Schumann, Jr.
Director of Planning
Fairfax County
Fairfax, Virginia

William L. Slayton
Assistant Director
National Association of Housing Officials
815 Seventeenth Street, N. W.
Washington 6, D. C.

Garland A. Wood
City Planner
City Planning Commission
217 Governor Street
Richmond 19, Virginia

Richard L. Steiner, Chairman
Director
Baltimore Redevelopment Commission
407-A Municipal Building
Baltimore 2, Maryland

Purpose

The Committee on City Planning Problems of the Central City and Suburban Fringe
was concerned with the most critical city planning problem faced by southern
cities today, the changing character and function of central areas and the unprecedented development of outlying sections. It attempted to recommend policies
and procedures for overcoming that problem and to suggest the research and ex-
perimentation which is still needed as a basis for formulating further policies
and procedures to solve it.

I

Findings

The major objective of city planning is the improvement of the physical and
cultural milieu constituting the urban complex. This improvement may be viewed
as threefold in nature:

1. Making the city a good place in which to live;

2. Providing an efficient place for business activities;

3. Furnishing facilities for pleasant recreation.

It is the task of city planning to see that this objective is achieved by the
most efficient and economical means commensurate with the principles of sound
governmental practices. A further timely objective is the reduction of the
potentialities of bomb damage, saving of life, and strengthening resistance to
further attack in the event of future wars involving this country.[1] These highly

---

1. A supplementary statement on this objective was prepared by Mr. Tracy
Augur, a member of the Committee on City Planning Problems of the Central City
and Suburban Fringe, and an outstanding expert in the field of urban vulnerability. That statement immediately follows the report of the Committee.

desirable goals of urban betterment can be achieved by the judicious employment
of city planning as a tool rather than an end in itself.

With these thoughts in mind, the Committee made a preliminary identification of
a number of city planning problems of the central city and suburban fringe.
Further analysis of these problems indicated their relative importance and the
fact that greater emphasis could be given to the most critical problems by
arranging them in five somewhat generalized groups.

The problems initially identified are summarized below, without any attempt to
place them in logical groupings or in the order of relative importance:

1. Expressways versus utilization of existing street
   pattern.

   a. need for and location of expressways
   b. consideration to mass transit in developing
      expressways
   c. relationship to central city and off-street
      parking facilities
   d. financing limitations
   e. border and access control

2. Railroad rerouting and terminal consolidation.

3. Relationship between off-street parking and building
   bulk in central areas.

   a. parking facilities on fringe of central
      areas and relationship to public transit.

4. Evaluating and determining areas for demolition,
   rehabilitation, and conservation.

5. Reduction of cost and time delays in urban redevelopment.

   a. can cost be reduced by code enforcement or
      by some method of forced amortization of
      structures?

6. What are desirable density standards for rebuilding
   central areas and developing outlying sections, and
   how can they best be enforced?

7. Is there an optimum size city, and if so how can
   growth beyond this point be prevented?

77

8. Industrial development.

    a. when and under what circumstances is it desirable?
    b. how should it be related to other land uses, the
       labor pool, and transportation?

9. How, and to what extent, should city planning policies
   and procedures be adjusted in recognition of the atomic
   age?

10. How can suburban land development best be controlled and
    reservations of land for public use be assured?

11. Shopping centers.

    a. relation to markets
    b. design standards
    c. problems resulting from granting franchises
       to some owners and denying them to others.

12. How can city planning become more effective in capital
    improvement budgeting, and how can capital improvement
    budgeting become more effective in civic improvement?

13. Decentralization.

    a. sociological and economic motivation
    b. attempts to influence decentralization

14. Metropolitan government.

    a. annexation
    b. the central city's policy on utilities for fringe
       areas. Inadequacy of inter-departmental and inter-
       governmental coordination in planning, etc.

15. Smoke and nuisance abatement as related to industrial
    control and planning.

16. Location of airports in relation to central city and
    land-use controls of adjacent land.

17. Economic deterioration of central areas.

18. Lack of long-range advance planning.

Careful examination of these problems and their further implications, particu-

larly toward the end of identifying those problems which are currently most

critical, resulted in five major classifications which the balanced judgment

of the Committee considered most important for the attention of responsible

southern leadership in the immediate future. These problem areas are:

2. Restricted mobility of people and goods

3. Obsolescence and deterioration of older central
   areas

4. Development of the suburban fringe

5. Administrative implementation.

II

Committee Conclusions

1. Problems resulting from the changing pattern of southern cities and assoc-
iated trends of decentralization, expansion, and urbanization are basic and
underlie all other critical city planning problems in the South today.

The South, long a predominantly rural area, is now being urbanized at a rapid
rate. At the same time, the traditional structure of its cities is undergoing
fundamental changes in response to new technological developments and living
habits. These two forces are producing great expansions in urban development,
often in forms that create difficult and unnecessary problems of government,
public services, economic stability, and national security. This expansion is
likely to continue for an indefinite period, probably at an accelerating rate,
leading to an intensification of these problems unless improved measures of
guidance are speedily developed and adopted.

2. Post-war growth in the number of automobiles has caused an over-crowding of
streets and parking facilities which has resulted in a loss of man-hours, increased cost of vehicle operation, and the depreciation of downtown taxable
values. Parking facilities and truck unloading zones have not increased in
proportion to the rise in motor vehicle use. Competition with an ever-increasing
number of automobiles for passengers and street space, together with the frequent
failure of city officials to recognize the importance of mass transportation,

has resulted in relatively fewer transit riders and thus a lessening of the
ability of mass transit to help solve the traffic problem.

3. Aging central areas of slums, blight, obsolete structures, and mixed uses
are evidence of cities' inability to adjust to present day needs. These un-
economic areas have saddled cities with land-use patterns that choke development. The function of these areas has changed, but not the structures or the
land-use pattern. Obsolete land-use patterns and structures are utilized for
activities for which they are unsuited, and the outmoded street patterns serve
as bottlenecks to traffic.

Many of these areas occupy desirable building sites, but the cost of the land
and structures, the inability on the part of a potential purchaser to change
the environment or land pattern, and the accessibility of urban fringe sites at
lower cost without these adverse factors are effective deterrents to the rebuilding of these areas.

Such areas are an economic drain upon the city. They still require municipal
servicing but provide little municipal revenue.

Some of the structures in such areas, though partially obsolete, are in an
adaptable land-use pattern and can be utilized through the rehabilitation process. Others are so structurally unsound and/or are in such an unadaptable land
pattern, that their continued use is a liability to the city's welfare.

4. There exists a critical land-use problem in the suburban fringe of growing
and expanding southern cities. Where land-use is unplanned and uncontrolled,
the land is frequently being used and developed for residential, commercial, and
industrial purposes in a manner which is inharmonious and economically burden-
some to whatever governmental jurisdiction is obliged to serve the area. The
haphazard development of residential land results in problems and deficiencies

relating to schools, public utilities, and other municipal services. Shopping facilities are being built in conflict with residential land-use and located along highways and at principal intersections so as to interfere with the efficient and safe use of those facilities. Industry seeking cheaper land and larger sites is too frequently being objectionably intermixed with residential developments, with serious effect on residential amenities, traffic facilities, and capacity of utilities.

Fringe development is a natural result of urban growth and expansion. Such development can be healthy and desirable if properly directed.

5. In many localities there is an evident lack of adequate coordination in planning between the various elements which comprise the physical plant of the community. This situation may result from a poor organizational form or administration of local planning or from the failure of the planning agency to establish sufficient stature and prestige in local government.

Another serious problem in this category is the frequent failure of communities to realize maximum benefit from such funds as become available from time to time for capital public improvements. This may often be attributed to failure to relate the expenditure of such funds to sound city planning.

The rapid expansion of southern cities has created the further problem of metropolitan area planning, as cities often find their urban areas extending beyond their corporate boundaries. Since the planning authority of a city usually does not extend beyond its corporate limits, nor permit it to plan in adjacent municipalities, it frequently happens that planning in areas outside the city limits is not coordinated with the central city's plan or that there is no planning at all in such areas. There is no mechanism in most metropolitan areas to assure comprehensive planning for the metropolitan or regional areas as a whole.

81

III

Recommendations

Recommendation No. 1

It is urgent that procedures be developed and adopted for assuring careful planning and control of urban development both within existing corporate limits of cities and in outside areas that are becoming, or are likely to become, urbanized.

Recommendation No. 2

Research should be instituted to determine at the earliest practicable date:

a. the most effective and economical pattern of urbanization for the South as a whole and for individual states, taking into account the proper servicing of the entire area with urban activities, the proper geographic distribution of economic opportunity, the proper balance of agriculture with other forms of gainful occupation, and the avoidance of conditions tending to invite enemy attack.

b. the upper and lower limits of size for individual cities to insure proper functioning of the local economy and the provision of satisfactory living and working conditions for the citizens.

c. the most effective and desirable developmental pattern for large urban areas to insure the optimum combination of sound living and working conditions and reasonable security from enemy attack.

Recommendation No. 3

Research should also be initiated to determine the exact nature of and the motivations for current trends in urban expansion in the South and the extent to which they contribute to the objectives determined as desirable in the preceding research project.

Recommendation No. 4

As soon as any of the research listed in Recommendation No. 2 produces significant and useful findings they should be disseminated to all groups engaged in

city planning or development and steps taken to secure their adoption.

Recommendation No. 5

Pending completion of needed research, all possible steps should be taken to avoid the accentuation of existing urban concentrations that are especially vulnerable to attack and the creation of new concentrations falling in that category. To that end, location of new industrial plants should be favored in small cities or otherwise removed a safe distance from urban centers that are now classified or seem likely to become classified as potential targets, and densities of new urban development should be held below levels that would create profitable targets.

Recommendation No. 6

Planners, and others concerned with improving the traffic situation, should recognize that the efficient and speedy movement of people and goods is essential to the over-all prosperity and growth of urban areas. This aim can be accomplished by recognizing that:

    a. It is the movement of people and goods, not merely the movement of vehicles, that is important. Mass transit not only utilizes street space more efficiently than automobiles, but also requires no downtown parking facilities, and therefore its use should be encouraged.

    b. Streets are primarily intended for the movement of vehicles and people, and not for vehicle storage. Parking should thus be prohibited on streets where it interferes with the orderly movement of vehicles.

    c. Expressways are important to the speedy movement of automobiles, trucks and busses, but must be accompanied by adequate downtown off-street parking and unloading facilities.

    d. Bulk and use zoning controls, combined with off-street parking and unloading facilities, are important tools for insuring that the demand of the central business district does not exceed the capacity of the transportation routes and vehicles to serve it.

83

Recommendation No. 7

There must be a careful study of aging central areas to determine their proper function, their proper land use pattern, their proper density. The city must develop a plan for a positive program for treating those areas. This program should include:

a. ways and means of clearing and rebuilding of those areas where the land pattern is unadaptable, the structural condition is beyond repair, and/or the land use is in conflict with current and probable future needs.

b. ways and means of rehabilitating those areas where the land use pattern can be changed to meet present and future needs, where the structures are subject to repair, and where continuation of the existing land use is in accord with the city's master plan.

c. conservation of structures and neighborhoods in areas where there is evidence of deterioration beginning so that these areas will not sink to conditions requiring more drastic treatment.

d. low rent housing for those families with incomes so low that they are forced to live in substandard structures.

Recommendation No. 8

To secure healthy and desirable fringe development, the following are recommended:

a. a positive plan for residential development implemented by the provision of municipal services and controls,

b. planned centers for shopping services and places of assembly, provided with off-street parking, accessible to various modes of transportation, and avoiding conflict with major traffic movement,

c. adequate land areas planned and protected for use by compatible industries, properly related to transportation, utilities, and labor supply.

Recommendation No. 9

Planning should be coordinated as thoroughly as possible between the official planning body and the action and operating departments of local government, such as schools, parks, public works, etc., and planning agencies should endeavor to gain the respect and confidence of their communities and local legislative bodies.

endation No. 10

l improvement budgeting should be a responsibility of community planning,
nds should not be expended for capital improvements until after receipt of
s from local planning agencies.

endation No. 11

ive mechanisms for planning and land development control on a metropoli-
regional basis should be developed in every such area as quickly as
le, regardless of political boundaries. Solutions, which cannot be
rdized for all localities, may include annexation, metropolitan or regiona
ng commissions, or the delegation of certain local governmental functions
ropolitan or regional governmental agencies.

85

Supplementary Statement to the Report of the
Committee on
City Planning Problems of the Central City and Suburban Fringe

by Tracy B. Augur
Urban Vulnerability Specialist
Executive Office of the President

The urban metropolis is rapidly becoming the dominant factor in the life of the
South, as it has previously become in the industrial Northeast, the Midwest and
the Pacific Coast. Over 80 per cent of the South's entire growth during the
1940 - 1950 decade took place in its larger metropolitan areas.

The emphasis on big city growth would present problems of city and state
planning serious enough in ordinary times. But these are not ordinary times.
We live in an age of peril such as the United States has never before experienced, and in that age the increasingly dominant position of the South's big
cities is an ominous source of danger both to the South and to the Nation of
which it is a part.

The outstanding fact of this age is that the more highly a nation's economic
and political life is concentrated in big cities, the more easily that nation
can be destroyed by an aggressor armed with modern weapons.

One need examine only a few simple statistics to realize that in those terms
this country is extremely vulnerable. Forty per cent of its population and
over fifty per cent of those employed in manufacturing are concentrated in just
40 metropolitan areas. Twelve of those areas are in the South.

All ordinary planning problems of city and suburb pale before the primary one
of reducing this high degree of concentration in big cities. As that problem
is solved, many of the others will disappear through gradual reduction of the
congestion of human activity that is their chief cause. Unless that problem
is solved, all other problems that beset the modern metropolis may be dissolved

in the blast and fire of nuclear explosions.

Each problem of central city and suburban fringe takes on a different aspect when viewed in that light. For example, the problem of city traffic becomes not one of filtering increasing numbers of people and vehicles through ever more congested business and residential areas, but of devising networks of fast arteries that will enable clusters of highly dispersed small cities to perform the economic, social and cultural functions of the modern metropolis.

Before detailed solutions to metropolitan problems can be examined fruitfully, it is necessary to devise basic patterns of urban life that deny to modern aggressors the kinds of targets that would need to cripple or destroy this country. When such patterns are set as goals, then measures of detailed city planning and land use control can be fitted to them, but until that is done detailed solutions are apt to be misdirected and, hence, wasteful of energy and resources.

CHAPTER X

PLANNING LEGISLATION AND ADMINSTRATION

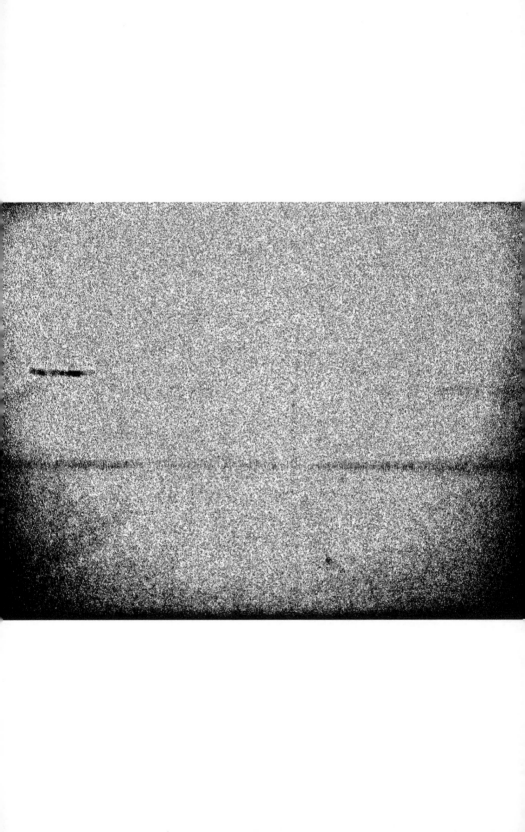

87

COMMITTEE ON PLANNING LEGISLATION AND ADMINISTRATION

Committee Members

Carter, Executive Director
unty Planning and Zoning
ssion
11
, Georgia

ook, Director
unty Planning Board
Florida

Cooper, Associate Director
of Public Administration
nda
ity of Virginia
tesville, Virginia

n T. Hedden
g and Zoning Consultant
14th Street, N. E.
, Georgia

on Hoffman
on Hoffman, Incorporated
g Consultants
syth Building
, Georgia

Arthur S. Owens, City Manager
Municipal Building
Roanoke, Virginia

W. B. Simmons
Jacksonville City Planning Advisory Board
c/o City Building Department
Jacksonville, Florida

Julian W. Tarrant
Consulting City Planner
900 West 31st Street
Richmond 25, Virginia

David R. Topp
Chief Zoning Inspector
City of Miami Beach
City Hall
Miami Beach, Florida

Jess Yarborough
County Commissioner
Chairman, Planning Zoning Building
   Commission
Miami, Florida

Philip P. Green, Jr., _Chairman_
Assistant Director
Institute of Government
University of North Carolina
Chapel Hill, North Carolina

88

REPORT

Purpose

The Committee on Planning Legislation and Administration regarded as its field
of inquiry the entire range of planning legislation, the administration of
planning programs under this legislation, and the impact of existing patterns
of governmental structure upon both planning legislation and administration.
It sought to identify those places at which positive action could be undertaken
to correct defects in these fields (either on a state or regional basis), the
forms such action might take, and matters concerning which further research is
necessary before any action program can be initiated.

I

Findings

The Committee believes that the importance to any planning program of adequate
legislative authority and of effective administration in all its phases is beyond question. As a starting point in its deliberations, the Committee made
an examination of the existing planning legislation in the South. The data
resulting from that examination is tabulated in Table I, at the conclusion of
the Committee report. A glance at the table makes it obvious that planning
enabling legislation in the southern states can only be described as being
"spotty." In many instances, local governmental units of a particular state
lack even the basic powers considered essential to any successful planning program. In other cases the planning legislation is generally inclusive, but
experience in these cases has indicated that certain provisions should be
modified so as to be made more effective.

89

The Committee studied the record of the adoption of uniform state laws by southern states and found that there has not been great enthusiasm for that approach. The record of uniform laws enacted by the southern states follows the Committee report as Table 2.

II

Committee Conclusions

The Committee considered ways and means of encouraging each of the southern states to adopt a basic set of planning laws. It decided that the most effective measure which could be undertaken on a regional basis would be the drafting of a new "model" act which could be copied, with necessary modifications, by the different states. While recognizing that existing model laws, such as the Standard City Planning Enabling Act and those acts prepared by Bettman and Bassett, represent an outstanding contribution to the city planning movement, the Committee believes that they should be subjected to reexamination in the light of the operating experience, new techniques, and court decisions of the past twenty years.

The Committee decided that at least one agency in each state should gather and make available information concerning planning laws, ordinances, court decisions and effective administrative practices. Such agencies are not present in every southern state today. The Committee believes that an organization similar to the Florida Planning and Zoning Association is an effective medium for disseminating such information. The Committee considered the desirability of establishing such a service agency on a regional basis, but it concluded that aside from such activities as those carried on by the Southern Association of State Planning and Development Agencies, there is no necessity for such an agency between the level of the states and the national planning service agencies.

90

The Committee concluded that a certain amount of research into the possibilities
of interstate cooperation in handling regional problems encountered in planning,
problems arising from defective governmental structure, the possibility of consolidating the several types of property controls now in existence, and procedures followed in administering planning controls needed to be done. It
considered also the possibility of research into comparative advantages and dis-
advantages of various types of administrative organization and procedures. It
concluded, however, that there are so many variables affecting the types of
organization and procedures used that such research would not be fruitful.

III

Recommendations

Recommendation No. 1

<u>That a new "model" planning enabling act for local governments in the southern</u>
<u>states be drafted.</u>

The Committee suggests that the drafting of this act be undertaken by an agency
in the South, with particular attention to southern conditions and needs. The
Committee considered the possibility of asking a national agency, such as the
American Society of Planning Officials, American Institute of Planners, or the
Commission   on Uniform State Laws, to prepare such an act. While it feels that
a nationwide act would not differ widely from one prepared solely for southern
states, it believes that the time consumed would not be adequately repaid in the
product.

The Committee recommends that there be wide discussion of the contents of the
proposed act by planners, lawyers, city and county officials, and other interested persons from each of the 14 southern states before its adoption in final
form. However, it suggests that a time limit of one year be set for delivery

inal product.

...ittee recommends that the following features be kept in mind in the ...g of this act:

1. It should be simple.

   The Committee feels that most existing planning legislation is unnecessarily verbose and that it goes into
   more detail than is desirable or necessary. In view
   of the increasing acceptance of planning by the courts,
   it is believed that a greatly simplified act would now
   be upheld.

2. It should be permissive, rather than mandatory.

   The Committee believes that local governmental units
   should have broad discretion as to the powers which they
   wish to exercise. While recognizing that mandatory provisions in some state legislation (e.g., Massachusetts,
   California) have resulted in establishment of planning
   agencies by a higher percentage of local governments, the
   Committee feels that better over-all results will be
   attained when a community is given its choice as to whether
   or not it wishes a planning program.

3. It should consist of a single, consolidated act, rather
   than a set of acts.

   Members of the Committee reported that the practice of
   spreading planning powers over a variety of acts scattered
   through the statute books has led to unnecessary confusion
   on the part of citizens and officials attempting to operate
   a coordinated planning program.

4. It should include the grant of authority to extablish a
   planning agency and make expenditures for planning, to
   enact zoning controls, including airport zoning, to regulate subdivisions, to adopt an official map, and to prepare
   capital expenditures budgets.

   The Committee agreed at the outset that the model act should
   include only those powers which are basic to any planning
   program. After due consideration of the various types of
   legislation which have been denoted from time to time as
   "planning legislation", the Committee decided that the above
   powers fall within this category of "basic" legislation.
   It recommends that the drafting agency consider expanding
   the scope of the usual authority for establishment of an
   official map so as to permit protection of sites for future
   parks and other public facilities as well as future streets.

5. It should grant such authority to municipalities, counties,
   and such regional planning agencies as local governmental
   units may establish by agreement among themselves.

92

The Committee recognizes that the greatest need for planning controls in the South at present is in the "fringe areas" surrounding city and town limits. The Committee believes that the utmost flexibility should be given to local governmental units in their efforts to deal with this problem. It believes that, generally speaking, better results will be attained through "grass roots" coordination by these units than by a solution imposed either by legislation or by a state agency.

6. It should give local governments discretion as to what type of administrative organization for planning they will use.

In its examination of existing state legislation, the Committee noted that virtually all of the state-wide acts require establishment of a planning board or planning commission before a local governmental unit can undertake a planning program. While recognizing the merits of such boards, the Committee feels that they are not always essential to the success of a planning program. Consequently, it recommends that the model act be flexible in this respect.

7. It should make provision for interim measures to handle emergency situations but should otherwise require that a planning agency be established and that planning activity take place before planning controls become effective.

The Committee recognizes that in many instances planning controls are imposed to meet immediately threatening situations. While it believes that such controls should be available for quick use when necessary, it believes that in the ordinary situation an adequate factual basis should be laid before any regulations are imposed upon the use of private property. It believes that such a basis is unlikely in the absence of a thorough planning program.

8. It might include provisions allowing a state agency to exercise temporary controls in particular areas to meet emergency growth situations where local governments have not yet acted.

In recent years the South has seen a number of instances in which rapid, unguided development has taken place while local governmental units were financially or administratively unable to cope with the situation. Although the Committee feels that as a general rule planning activity under this act should be carried on by local governments, it recognizes that it might be wise to authorize state agencies to take emergency action of limited duration where such situations arise.

93

Committee **rec**ommends further that the model act be made available to inter-
d persons and organizations in each state, as a guide for new legislation.

Committee has considered various techniques of presenting legislation to
e legislatures, including the possibility of submitting the act to the
hern Governors' Conference for the purpose of securing support. It believes
such legislation is more apt to be adopted if it is requested by local
rnmental units, rather than imposed from above. Consequently, the Committee
eves that this matter should be left in the hands of interested persons and
nizations in each of the various states, with no attempt on a region-wide
s to "push" the legislation.

general rule, the Committee believes that the best approach to the state
slature is through the cooperative efforts of state Leagues of Municipali-
, Associations of County Commissioners, and statewide planning organizations.

Committee recognizes that in some situations enactment of this legislation
be feasible only on a "special act" basis for one or a few governmental
s. Consequently, the act should be made available not only to statewide
nizations but also to any other agencies which might assist specific com-
ties with their problems.

mmendation No. 2

the formation of statewide planning associations in each state be encour-
, as a means of dissemination of information concerning planning laws,
nances, court decisions, and effective administrative practices.

mmendation No. 3

research be undertaken concerning the following matters:

    1. Problems and procedures involved in securing interstate
       cooperation in handling regional problems, such as the
       development in the vicinity of the Savannah River projects.

94

2. Problems resulting from defective governmental structure and means of solving them (annexation, extraterritorial jurisdiction, city-county consolidation, special districts, etc.).

3. Means of consolidating at the local level the various types of property controls which are presently scattered through a variety of regulations.

4. Compilation of procedures which are followed in administering planning controls, for the benefit of local citizens.

95

TABLE 1

SELECTED PLANNING LEGISLATION IN THE SOUTHERN STATES[1]

	Ala	Ark	Fla	Ga	Ky	La	Md	Miss	NC	Okla	SC	Tenn	Tex	Va
Enabling Acts														
	*			*	*	*	*		*	*	x	*		*
ty												*		
	x			x	x	*	*		*	x	x			*
	*			x	*		x		*	x	x	*-		*
	*	*	*	*	*	*	*		*	*	*	*		*
abling Acts														
	*	*	*	*	*	*	*	*	*	*	*	*	*	*
l	x	x	x	x			*		x	x	x	*		*
							..				x			
on Control														
	~	*		*	*	*	*	*	*	*	x	*	*	*
l	x	*				*	*		*		x		*	*
							x				x			
	*	*	*	*		*	*	*	*	x				
eets Acts														
				*	x	*		x	x	x				
						*		x	x					
cess Streets	*		*		*	*	*						*	*
thorities	*	*	*	*	*	*	*	*	*		*	*	*	*
velopment	*	*	*#	*#	*	*	x		*		*	*		*
using Stds.				*	*				*		*	*		
ning	*	*		*	*	*	*	*	*	*	*	*	*	

ons for the planning legislation now operative in the fourteen states are
in succeeding pages.

Legend
* General Law
x Special act applying to one or a few
  governmental subdivisions
Act held unconstitutional

96

SELECTED PLANNING LEGISLATION IN THE SOUTHERN STATES

(citations are to Code of Alabama, 1940, as amended)

nning Boards or Commissions
  City: Tit. 37, ss. 786-797 (any municipality)
  County: Tit. 62, ss. 330(204)-330(213) (over 400,000 pop.)
  Regional: Tit. 37, ss. 809-814
  State: Tit. 55, ss. 373(1)-373(6)

ing
  City: Tit. 37, ss. 9, 772-785, 796 (any municipality); Tit. 62,
      s. 594 (Montgomery & Mobile), ss. 710-720 (Birmingham)
  County: Tit. 62, ss. 330(230)-330(242) (over 400,000 pop.),
      s. 330(243) (county over 300,000 may zone unzoned cities
      within its boundaries)

division Regulation
  City: Tit. 37, ss. 797-803 (any municipality & 5 miles beyond)
  County: Tit. 37, s. 797; Tit. 62, ss. 330(204), 330(214)-330(220)
      (over 400,000 pop.)
  State: Tit. 56, ss. 12-25

ped Streets
  City: Tit. 37, ss. 804-808 (any municipality)
  County: Tit. 62, ss. 330(221)-330(229) (over 400,000 pop.)

ited Access Streets & Highways
  Tit. 36, ss. 1(15), 58(11), 58(12)

sing Authorities
  Tit. 25, ss. 1-95

an Redevelopment
  Tit. 25, ss. 96-104

port Zoning
  Tit. 4, s. 33

er
  Industrial Development Boards: Tit. 37, ss. 815-830

s (citations are to Arkansas Statutes Annotated, 1947, as amended)

nning Boards or Commissions
  City: Tit. 19, ss. 19-2811 to 19-2819 (over 1,750 pop. & 5 miles beyond)
  County: Tit. 17, ss. 17-1101 to 17-1106 (any county)
  State: Tit. 9, ss. 9-301 to 9-305 (Arkansas Resources Development Comm.)

ing
  City: Tit. 19, ss. 19-2804 to 19-2810 (any municipality)
  County: Acts, 1952, c._____ (over 150,000 pop.)

g (cont.)

ivision Regulation
City: Tit. 19, s. 19-2816 (any municipality & 5 miles beyond)
County: Tit. 17, s. 17-1106 (any county)
State: Tit. 17, ss. 17-1201 to 17-1211; Tit. 19, ss. 19-401 to 19-413

ped Streets
City: Tit. 19, ss. 19-2808 to 19-2810, 19-2813(b), 19-2816 (setback lines)

sing Authorities
Tit. 19, ss. 19-3001 to 19-3074

an Redevelopment
Tit. 19, ss. 19-3056 to 19-3063

port Zoning
Tit. 74, ss. 74-301 to 74-307

(citations are to Florida Statutes Annotated, as amended)

nning Boards or Commissions
State: Chapter 420 (Florida State Improvement Commission)

ing
City: Chapter 176, ss. 176.01 to 176.24 (any municipality)
County: No general law, but special acts authorize zoning by at least
18 counties.

ivision Regulation
State: Chapter 177, ss. 177.01 to 177.15; Chapter 192, s. 192.56

ited Access Streets & Highways
Chapter 348

sing Authorities
Chapters 421, 422, 423

an Redevelopment
Chapter 421, s. 421.08 (Acts, 1945, c. 23077, as amended by Acts, 1949,
c. 26477, and Acts, 1951, c. 27091) /Held unconstitutional in Adams
v. Housing Authority, 60 S.2d 63 (1952)7

(citations are to Georgia Code Annotated, as amended, except where
otherwise indicated)

nning Boards or Commissions
City: Tit. 69, ss. 69-801 to 69-843 (any municipality)
Metropolitan: Laws, 1947, No. 230 (Fulton & DeKalb Counties)
County: Tit. 69, s. 808 (municipal Planning Commission may be designated
as County Planning Commission); Laws, 1947, No. 15 (pop.
81,000-82,000)

98

Georgia (cont.)

Planning Boards or Commissions
 Regional: Tit. 69, s. 69-804 (joint city-county commission); Laws,
  1949, No. 101 (Warm Springs Memorial Area, Meriwether,
  Harris, Talbot Counties)
 State: Tit. 40, ss. 40-2101 to 40-2120 (Department of Commerce)

Zoning
 City: Tit. 69, ss. 69-810 to 69-835, 69-9903 (any municipality)
 County: No general law, but a number of special acts for particular
  counties.

Subdivision Regulation
 City: Tit. 69, ss. 69-837 to 69-839 (any municipality)
 State: Tit. 24, s. 24-2716

Housing Authorities
 Tit. 99, ss. 99-1101 to 99-1173

Urban Redevelopment
 Tit. 99, ss. 99-1201a to 99-1215a /Held unconstitutional in Housing
 Authority v. Johnson, 74 S.E.2d 891 (1953)/

Airport Zoning
 Tit. 11, ss. 11-401 to 11-422, 11-9902

Kentucky (citations are to Kentucky Revised Statutes, 1948, as amended)

Planning Boards or Commissions
 City: Chapter 100, ss. 100.010 to 100.990 (any municipality over
  100,000 & 5 miles beyond, any municipality between 20,000-
  100,000 & 3 miles beyond, any other municipality); Chapter
  147, ss. 147.190 to 147.250 (Frankfort)
 County: See above citation for city, for authority for joint city-
  county Planning Commission for county containing city of
  over 100,000 population
 Regional: Chapter 147, ss. 147.130 to 147.180
 State: Chapter 147, ss. 147.260 to 147.310 (Agricultural & Industrial
  Development Board)

Zoning
 City: Chapter 100, ss. 100.066 to 100.086 (over 100,000 pop.), ss.
  100.390 to 100.490 (20,000-100,000 pop.), ss. 100.500 to 100.600
  (under 20,000), ss. 100.970 to 100.990; Chapter 147, ss. 147.190
  to 147.250 (Frankfort)

Subdivision Regulation
 City: Chapter 100, ss. 100.010, 100.087 to 100.094 (over 100,000 pop.
  & 5 miles beyond), ss. 100.360 (20,000-100,000 pop. & 3 miles
  beyond), ss. 100.720 to 100.780 (under 20,000 pop. & 5 miles
  beyond), ss. 100.970 to 100.990

Mapped Streets
 City: Chapter 100, s. 100.076 (over 100,000), ss. 100,790 to 100,830
  (under 20,000 pop.)

(citations are to Annotated Code of Maryland, Flack, 1951, as amended)

ning Boards or Commissions
City: Art. 66B, ss. 10-20, 34-37 (any municipality)
County: Art. 66B, ss. 10-20, 34-37 (any county)
Regional: Laws, 1927, c. 448 as amended (Maryland-Washington Metropolitan
            District)
State: Art. 88C, ss. 1-8

ng
City: Art. 66B, ss. 1-9 (Baltimore & towns over 10,000 pop.), ss. 21-23
       (all but Baltimore)
County: Art. 66B, ss. 21-23 (any county). There are also special
         acts for a number of counties.
Regional: Laws, 1943, c. 992; Laws, 1927, c. 448 (Maryland-Washington
            Metropolitan District)

division Regulation
City: Art. 66B, ss. 10, 24-30 (all but Baltimore)
County: Art. 66B, ss. 10, 24-30 (any county)
Regional: Laws, 1927, c. 448; Laws, 1939, c. 714; Laws, 1943, c. 992
            (Maryland-Washington Metropolitan District)
State: Art. 17, ss. 71-75

ed Streets
City: Art. 66B, ss. 31-33 (all but Baltimore)
County: Art. 66B, ss. 31-33 (any county)

ted Access Streets & Highways
Art. 89B, ss. 32, 33, 18, 164-170

sing Authorities
Art. 44A, ss. 1-33; Art. 44B, ss. 1-10

an Redevelopment
Md. Const., Art. 11B. Laws, 1945, c. 1012; Laws, 1947, cs. 42, 162,
504; Laws, 1949, c. 217 (Baltimore only)

port Zoning
Art. 1A, s. 16

ppi   (citations are to Mississippi Code, 1942, as amended)

ng
City: ss. 3590-3597 (over 1,000 pop.)

division Regulation
City: s. 3374-123
State: ss. 4278-4283

sing Authorities
ss. 7295 to 7344-01

port Zoning
ss. 7544-01 to 7544-17

arolina   (citations are to General Statutes, 1943, as amended)

ning Boards or Commissions
City: G.S. 160-22 to 160-24 (any municipality)
County: G.S. 153-9(40) (any county)
Regional: G.S. 160-22, 153-9(40) (joint planning boards); Sess. Laws,
           1947, c. 677 (Winston-Salem/Forsyth County)
State: G.S. 143-171 to 143-177.1

ing
City: G.S. 160-172 to 160-181.1 (any municipality)
County: Sess. Laws, 1947, c. 677 (Forsyth); Sess. Laws, 1949, c. 1043
         (Durham); Sess. Laws, 1951, c. 1193 (Dare)

ivision Regulation
City: G.S. 160-226, 160-227 (any municipality & 1 mile beyond)
State: G. S. 39-28 to 39-32.4, 47-30

ed Streets
City: Pvt. Laws, 1927, c. 156 (Durham, Greensboro, Raleigh, Winston-
       Salem); Sess. Laws, 1947, c. 677, s. 11 (Winston-Salem/Forsyth
       County)

sing Authorities
G.S. Chapter 157

an Redevelopment
G.S. 160-454 to 160-474

mum Housing Standards
G.S. 160-182 to 160-191

ort Zoning
G.S. 63-29 to 63-37

   (citations are to Oklahoma Statutes Annotated, 1951, as amended)

ning Boards or Commissions
City: Tit. 11, ss. 421-425 (any municipality), ss. 1411-1435 (over
       160,000 pop.), ss. 1451-1473 (142,000-204,000 pop.)
County: Tit. 19, ss. 861.1-861.24 (100,000-244,000 pop.), ss. 865.1-
         865.25 (over 240,000 pop.)
Regional: Tit. 11, ss. 431-437; Laws, 1953, S.B. 353 (Tulsa Metro-
           politan Area)
State: Tit. 74, ss. 344.9-360.2 (Oklahoma Planning & Resources Board)

ing
City: Tit. 11, ss. 401-410 (any municipality)
County: Tit. 19, ss. 861.13-861.24 (100,000-244,000 pop.); ss. 865.3,
         865.11-865.21 (over 240,000 pop.)

division Regulation
    City: Tit. 11, ss. 406, 423 (any municipality), ss. 1423-1430 (over
           160,000 pop. & 3 miles beyond), ss. 1462-1469 (142,000-204,000
           pop. & 5 miles beyond)
    County: Tit. 19, s. 861.10 (100,000-244,000 pop.), s. 865.8 (over
           240,000 pop.)
    State: Tit. 11, ss. 511-532

ped Streets
    City: Tit. 11, ss. 1431-1435 (over 160,000 pop.), ss. 1470-1473
           (142,000-204,000 pop.)
    County: Tit. 19, ss. 865.9, 865.10 (over 240,000 pop.), ss. 861.11,
           861.12 (100,000-244,000 pop.)

port Zoning
    Tit. 3, ss. 101-115

arolina   (citations are to Code of Laws of South Carolina, 1952)

nning Boards or Commissions
    City: ss. 47-1021 to 47-1055 (over 34,000 pop.), ss. 47-1061 to 47-1094
           (15,250 to 16,000 pop. at 1940 census), ss. 47-1101 to 47-1113
           (Aiken & North Augusta)
    County: ss. 14-355 to 14-384 (counties containing city over 70,000
           pop.), ss. 14-391 to 14-399.6 (counties with "sudden influx of
           large numbers of prospective inhabitants")
    Regional: s. 14-359 (county containing city over 70,000 pop. plus other
           county or counties)
    State: ss. 9-301 to 9-312

ing
    City: ss. 47-1001 to 47-1017 (any municipality), s. 47-1048 (over
           34,000 pop.), s. 47-1094 (15,250-16,000 pop. & 3 miles beyond),
           ss. 47-1102 to 47-1106 (Aiken & N. Augusta)
    County: ss. 14-352 to 14-354, 14-361 to 14-365, 14-368 to 14-384 (over
           70,000 pop.), ss. 14-398 to 14-399.6 (counties with sudden influx
           of population)
    Regional: ss. 14-352 to 14-354, 14-359, 14-361 to 14-365, 14-368 to
           14-384

division Regulation
    City: ss. 47-1038 to 47-1055 (over 34,000 pop. & 3 miles beyond),
           ss. 47-1084 to 47-1094 (15,250-16,000 pop. & 3 miles beyond),
           s. 47-1329 (35,000 pop. & 5 miles beyond)
    County: ss. 14-366, 14-367 (over 70,000 pop.)
    Regional: ss. 14-359, 14-366, 14-367

ped Streets
    City: s. 47-1037 (over 34,000 pop.), s. 47-1093 (15,250-16,000 pop.)

sing Authorities
    ss. 36-1 to 36-307, 36-601 to 36-651

an Redevelopment
    ss. 36-401 to 36-414

nimum Housing Standards
   ss. 36-501 to 36-511

rport Zoning
   ss. 2-131 to 2-133 (in vicinity of U.S.A.F. base or field)

ee (citations are to Tennessee Code Annotated, Williams, 1934, as
   amended)

anning Boards or Commissions
   City: ss. 3493.1 to 3493.9 (any municipality)
   Community: ss. 552.24a to 552.24e
   Regional: ss. 552.14 to 552.24
   State: ss. 552.7 to 552.24e

ning
   City: ss. 3407.1 to 3407.9 (any municipality)
   County (regional): ss. 10268.1 to 10268.13

division Regulation
   City: ss. 3407.10 to 3407.19 (any municipality)
   Regional: ss. 3493.10 to 3493.20

using Authorities
   ss. 3647.1 to 3647.41

an Redevelopment
   ss. 3647.52 to 3647.63

nimum Housing Standards
   ss. 3647.42 to 3647.51

rport Zoning
   ss. 2726.47 to 2726.61

citations are to Texas Civil Statutes Annotated, Vernon, 1925, as
ended, except where otherwise indicated)

ing
   City: Arts. 1011a to 1011k (any municipality)

division Regulation
   City: Art. 974a (any municipality & 5 miles beyond); Vernon's Ann.
        Penal Code, Arts. 427b, 1137h
   County: Art. 6626

ped Streets
   City: Art. 1105a (over 15,000 pop., building lines)

ited Access Streets & Highways
   Art. 1085a

using Authorities
    Arts. 1269k to 1269l

rport Zoning
    Arts. 46e-1 to 46e-15

her
    Art. 6812b, ss. 7-9 (county highway planning, counties with 198,000-
    400,000 pop.)

a (citations are to Code of Virginia, 1950, as amended)

anning Boards or Commissions
    City: ss. 15-899 to 15-914 (any municipality)
    County: ss. 15-915 to 15-926.1 (any county)
    Regional: ss. 15-891.1 to 891.9; also s. 15-903 (joint municipal
              planning commissions)
    State: ss. 10-118 to 10-126 (Division of Planning & Economic
          Development)

ning
    City: ss. 15-819 to 15-843 (any municipality)
    County: ss. 15-10, 15-844 to 15-854 (any county), ss. 15-855 to
          15-885 (counties meeting certain statutory qualifications),
          ss. 15-886 to 15-890 (counties adjoining cities over
          180,000 pop.)

bdivision Regulation
    City: ss. 15-779 to 15-794.3 (incorporated towns & 2 miles beyond,
          cities under 100,000 pop. & 3 miles beyond, cities over 100,000
          pop. & 5 miles beyond; does not apply to any county adjacent to
          a county having pop. density of over 1,000 per square mile);
          ss. 15-796 to 15-806 (cities under 100,000 pop. & 3 miles beyond);
          ss. 15-807 to 15-818 (towns & 2 miles beyond)
    County: ss. 15-779 to 15-794.3 (does not apply to any county adjacent
          to a county having pop. density of over 1,000 per square
          mile), ss. 15-795 to 15-795.2 (counties exempted from above)

mited Access Streets & Highways
    ss. 15-7.1, 33-37 to 33-43

using Authorities
    ss. 36-1 to 36-69

ban Redevelopment
    ss. 36-48 to 36-55

her
    Advisory Council on the Virginia Economy: ss. 10-127 to 10-132

RECORD OF UNIFORM & MODEL STATE LAWS ENACTED

	U.S.	So.	Ala	Ark	Fla	Ga	Ky	La	Md	Miss	NC	Okla	SC	Tenn	Tex	Va
LAWS	1070	254	18	22	18	9	13	21	32	11	22	13	16	26	15	18
›le ›nts (96)	48	14	x	x	x	x	x	x	x	x	x	x	x	x	x	x
›e (06)	48	14	x	x	x	x	x	x	x	x	x	x	x	x	x	x
›e ›ts (22)	17	3	x				x		x							
›t (06)	34	5	x	x			x		x				x			
›t ›ts (22)	11	2	x											x		
›9)	31	6	x	x			x	x		x			x			
(09)	48	14	x	x	x	x	x	x	x	x	x	x	x	x	x	x
›n & ›rt (10)	19	4	x						x						x	x
›hip (14)	32	6		x					x	x			x	x		x
›hip (16)	35	7	.	x	x				x		x	x		x		x
(17)	17	5					x	x	x					x		x
›nt ›ces (18)	20	2							x				x			

Table II
RECORD OF UNIFORM & MODEL STATE LAWS ENACTED

	U.S.	So.	Ala	Ark	Fla	Ga	Ky	La	Md	Miss	NC	Okla	SC	Tenn	Tex	Va
FORM LAWS	1070	254	18	22	18	9	13	21	32	11	22	13	16	26	15	18
otiable truments (96)	48	14	x	x	x	x	x	x	x	x	x	x	x	x	x	x
ehouse eipts (06)	48	14	x	x	x	x	x	x	x	x	x	x	x	x	x	x
ehouse eipts ndments (22)	17	3	x					v			x					
es Act (06)	34	5	x	x												
es Act ndments (22)	11	2	x										x			
ls of ing (09)	31	6	x	x				x	x		x		x			
ck nsfer (09)	48	14	x	x	x	x	x	x	x	x	x	x	x	x	x	x
ertion & support (10)	19	4	x													
tnership (14)	32	6		x				x		x		x	x			x
ited tnership (16)	35	7	·	x	x			x		x	x		x			x
g Act (17)	17	5					x	x	x				x			x
udulent veyances (18)	20	2														
of of tutes (20)	27	4														
eign ositions (20)	13	4														
laratory gments (22)	37	11	x	x	x	x		x	x		x		x	x	x	x
uciaries (22)	21	4	x					x	x	x						
eral Tax Lien gistration (26)	23	6		x			x	x	x							
ciprocal Trans- r Tax (28)	17	2														
terans' Guard- ship (28)	40	12	x	x	x	x	x	x	x	x	x	x	x	x		
terans' ardianship endments (42)	19	5		x			x		x	x			x			
incipal & come (31)	17	7	x		x			x				‥	‥			
secure tendance of t-of-state tnesses (31)	42	11		x	x		x		x	x	x	x	x	x	x	x	

Law	U.S.	So.	Ala	Ark	Fla	Ga	Ky	La	Md	Miss	NC	Okla	SC	Tenn	Tex	Va
Marcotic Drug (32)	44	14	:	–	x	–	–	x	x	–	–	x	–	–	x	–	x
Narcotic Drug Amendments (42)	5	1						x								
Trust Receipts (33)30	5				x			x	x							c
Transfer of Dependents (35)	9	1						x								
Vendor & Purchaser Risk (35)	6	0														
Criminal Extradition (36)	36	9	x				x		x		:		x		x	:
Business Records as Evidence (36)	20	2		x			x				:		x		x	:
Judicial Notice of Foreign Laws (36)	26	5				x			x			x		x	:
Official Reports as Evidence (36)	6	1					x									x
Trustee's Accounting (36)	5	0														
Trusts (37)	7	4			x	x	x		x	x	x		x		x	–
Property (38)	1	0														
Unauthorized Insurers (38)	7	4	c		x	x	x		x	c						
Common Trust Fund (38)	21	6	:		x	x		x						x	
Absentees' Property (39)	3	2				x	x				x				x	
Acknowledgment (39)25	3		x	x								x				
Acknowledgment Amendment (42)	21	2	x		x	x	x		x				x		x	
Participation by Secured Creditors (39)	5	0														
Joint Tort-feasors (39)	10	3		x		x	x		x				x		x	
Insurers Liquidation (39)	12	4			x	x	x		x				x		x	
Statute of Limitations (39)	0	0														
Pistol (40)	2	0														
Simultaneous Death (40)	39	10			x	x	x		x				x		x	:
Vital Statistics (42)	10	3														

Law	U.S.	So.	Ala	Ark	Fla	Ga	Ky	La	Md	Miss	NC	Okla	SC	Tenn	Tex	Va
Arbitration of Death Taxes (44)	11	3												--	--	
Compromise of Death Taxes (44)	12	3													x	x
Powers of Foreign Representatives (44)	0	0														
Reverter of Realty (46)	-	-														
Divorce Recognition (47)	9	2					x						x			
Enforcement of Foreign Judgments (48)	7	1	x													
Ancillary Administration of Estates (49)	1															
Photographic Copies as Evidence (49)	21	6	x	x		x		x			x	x				
Marriage License Application (50)	0	0														
Prenatal Blood Test (50)	0	0														
Probate of Foreign Wills (50)	1	0														
Reciprocal Enforcement of Support (50)	38	12	x	x		x	x	x	x		x	x	x	x	x	x
Commercial Code (51)	1	0														
Blood Tests to Determine Paternity (52)	1	0														
Single Publication (52)	-	-														
Rules of Criminal Procedure (52)	0	0														
MODEL ACTS	44	12	1	1	0	0	1	1	3	1	0	1	0	2	1	0
Interparty Agreement (25)	4	1														
Joint Obligations (25)	4	0														
Written Obligations (25)	2	0														
Business Corporations (28)	5	»														
Composite Reports as Evidence (36)	3	0														
Expert Testimony (37)	2	0														

Uniform & Model State Laws——4,

Law	U.S.	So.	Ala	Ark	Fla	Ga	Ky	La	Md	Miss	MO	Okla	SC	Tenn	Tex	Va
Estates (38)	0	0														
Execution of Wills (40)	1	1														
Power of Sale Mortgage Foreclosure (40)	0	0														
Resale Price Control (40)	0	0														
Administration of Charitable Trusts (44)	2	1	—	—	—	—	—	—	—							
Rule against Perpetuities (44)	2	0							x			—	—	—		
Act for Appointment of Commissioners (44)	11	5	⌒													
War Service Validation (44)	1	0														
State Administrative Procedures Act (46)	3	0														
Court Administrator (48)	1	0										x				
Co-Pres (44)	2	1	—									—				
Small Estates (51)	0	0										—				
Anti-Gambling (52)	0	0														
Crime Investigating Commission (52)	0	0														
Department of Justice (52)	0	0														
Perjury (52)	1	0	—													
Police Council (52)	0	0														
State Witness Immunity (52)	0	0														

CHAPTER XI

CITY PLANNING AND INDUSTRIAL DEVELOPMENT

COMMITTEE ON CITY PLANNING AND INDUSTRIAL DEVELOPMENT

Committee Members

k A. Bagdon
, Director
f Labor Statistics
partment of Labor.
th Street, N. E.
5, Georgia

L. Beck, Executive Director
Roanoke Redevelopment and
g Authority
x 1807
, Virginia

R. Darragh, Manager
, Division
. Association of Manufacturers
ing Street, N. W.
Georgia

Robert J. Fuller, Chief
Requirements Branch
Division
f the Chief of Civil
s and Military Government
agon
on 25, D. C.

Robert M. Holder
Commercial and Industrial Real Estate
512 Title Building
Atlanta 3, Georgia

William A. Lufburrow
Industrial Representative
Georgia Department of Commerce
100 State Capitol
Atlanta, Georgia

Dorman W. Miller
Industrial Development Agent
Appalachian Power Company
Roanoke, Virginia

Henry C. Moore
Director of Planning
City-County Planning Board
Winston-Salem, North Carolina

Warren Zitzmann
Planning and Zoning Consultant
Agricultural and Industrial Development
Board
New Capitol Office Building
Frankfort, Kentucky

George W. Hubley, Jr., Chairman
Executive Director
Agricultural and Industrial Development Board
Frankfort, Kentucky

110

REPORT

Purpose

The Committee on City Planning and Industrial Development had as its purpose to
inquire into the planning considerations involved in a characteristic southern
community subject to industrial development, and to devise techniques for as-
certaining what the industries seeking to locate in southern communities have a
right to expect of those communities and what the communities have a right to
expect from the incoming industries.

I

Findings

Planning Commissions throughout the South are making valuable contributions to
industrial development and are playing a vital role in the development of this
industrial frontier. The coextensive nature of city planning and industrial
development needs to be emphasized, however, if sound community development is
to result. The rapid industrial growth of the South during the last decade
marks the evident need for scientific guidance to assure proper assimilation of
industrial development in the interest of a balanced economy and to maintain
the best of the traditions of the southern region.

II

Committee Conclusions

1. The Committee believes that a community has the right to expect that industry
   will accept its responsibility as an outstanding citizen and will take an
   active part in cultural and civic affairs.

111

2. The Committee believes that the continuation of industrial growth in the South must be insured so as constantly to improve urban environment in relation to economic and industrial expansion.

III

Recommendations

Recommendation No. 1

The Committee recommends to the Congress that the Regional Committee on City Planning encourage establishment of planning commissions on a municipal, county, and/or regional basis. These commissions must be manned with the most competent lay leadership available. The leadership should be of such caliber that it will engender the acceptance and trust of both incoming and local business and industrial leaders, civic leaders, governing bodies and citizens. It is further recommended that competent personnel be selected to staff these commissions and that they be qualified to guide the commission in the enlistment of cooperation and assistance of advisory committees selected from representatives of community-wide interests.

It is recognized that in order to do an effective job of contributing to a high rate of diversified industrial development in the community the commission should direct and assist its staff in maintaining a close and constant liaison with all appropriate departments of municipal, county and state governments as well as representative civic organizations.

Recommendation No. 2

The Committee recommends that the planning commission assume responsibility for the availability of data essential to industry in determining plant location, and, if necessary, that it stimulate the compilation of such data by the appropriate responsible agencies.

ld be the duty and responsibility of the established commission to review,
and assure the validity of established information available and/or to
te research for adequate information where lacking.

ld be the further responsibility of the Commission to be able to advise
uch information can be obtained.

ndation No. 3

mittee recommends that the planning commission recognize, concern itself
d lend encouragement to civic and municipal organizations to establish a
designed to relate and convey to opinion molding groups the economic
of selective industrial expansion.

responsible industry is interested in community attitudes, it becomes an
ion of the planning commission to study and assist the development of
ttitudes as an integral part of city planning responsibility.

nning commission can help to achieve this objective through development
own public relations program.

ndation No. 4

mittee recommends that the importance of planning to industrial develop-
stifies the rewriting and reproduction of this report or that portion of
interest to business and industrial leaders in a suitable form for dis-
on to business and industrial leaders throughout the South, and this
ee offers to assume the responsibility for this job.

ndation No. 5

mittee recommends that the Congress on City Planning recommend to the
Committee on City Planning action to review and study experiences of
porations of a diversified nature and size that have moved into a

ross-section of communities throughout the South in the last decade, to
e the required community facilities and services of these industries.
rther recommended that study and research be made of communities which
uired new industries to determine how these various communities met or
o meet these needs of industry for services.

lts of these case studies, when assembled, should be maintained on file
Regional Committee on City Planning and loaned or furnished upon request.
brary" of vital information would of course be of little value unless
stence, content and availability were made known to those individuals
cies concerned with city planning.

CHAPTER **XII**

STUDENT RECRUTIMENT AND UNDERGRADUATE PREPERATION

114

COMMITTEE ON STUDENT RECRUITMENT AND UNDERGRADUATE PREPARATION

<u>Committee Members</u>

L. Daugherty
t Paces Ferry Road, N. E.
5, Georgia

H. Dill, Director
re County Planning Commission
hington Avenue
4, Maryland

Dinwiddie, Dean
of Architecture
University
eans, Louisiana

ipziger-Pearce
Director
of Architecture
ity of Texas
12, Texas

M. Lester, Secretary
e Corporation of New York
ro Road
Hill, North Carolina

Malcolm G. Little, Jr.
Assistant Professor
School of Architecture
Georgia Institute of Technology
Atlanta, Georgia

Hubert B. Owens, Chairman
Department of Landscape Architecture
University of Georgia
Athens, Georgia

S. S. Steinberg, Dean
College of Engineering
University of Maryland
College Park, Maryland

James W. Webb, Associate Professor
Department of City and Regional
    Planning
University of North Carolina
Chapel Hill, North Carolina

Buford L. Pickens, <u>Chairman</u>
Dean
School of Architecture
Washington University
St. Louis 5, Missouri

<u>Purpose</u>

The Committee on Student Recruitment and Undergraduate Preparation defined its

purpose thus:

1. To explore the ways and means of attracting more well-qualified
   undergraduate students to graduate professional training in city
   planning in the South, and

2. To consider how various undergraduate programs can most effectively prepare interested students for such graduate professional
   training.

In view of the many surveys, reports and commentaries which have been and are now

being made with regard to the quality and quantity of graduate education in this

field, the Committee did not concern itself with this question, assuming that "no

graduate program can be any better than the quality of student attracted to it

from the undergraduate college."[1]

I

<u>Findings</u>

The unprecedented rate of urban expansion in the South and the urgent need[2] for

the services of competent city planners to guide the growth of existing urban

areas and the development of new ones are well known. The American Society of

Planning Officials this year reports that there are only one hundred new pro-

fessionally trained planners to fill two hundred vacancies and new positions.

Yet, in the face of this condition, the Committee noted an almost total lack of

---

1. John M. Gaus, in a paper presented at a Conference on Education for
Regional Planning and Development, University of North Carolina,   November, 1950.

2. See Table I immediately following this report for a graphic demonstration
of this need.

interest in, or knowledge of, city planning as a professional career on the part
of college students, teachers, department heads and deans. This situation is
complicated by the fact that there is no consensus in the United States as to
what constitutes desirable undergraduate preparation for city planners, or indeed,
as to what the basic qualifications for planners should be. In order to provide
a background of authoritative opinion on these subjects, the following commentaries
were solicited from various qualified sources by the Committee Chairmen and were
distributed to the working committee members prior to the Congress.

1. **From the director of a metropolitan planning commission:**

" I want to emphasize strongly that planning is primarily a
discipline involving man's relation to man and is not a profession in which mechanical techniques are of first importance.
I do not mean by this that planning is without techniques or
that a man can succeed in planning without the proper technical
tools. I do mean, however, that the planner's role is pre-
eminently that of understanding other people's points of view,
rationalizing conflicts, catalyzing situations, developing programs out of diverse opinions, exciting others to action on the
basis of common goals and in general dealing with people and
their attitudes. So many planners that we turn out are tech-
nically competent and philosophically sterile.

"I would urge strongly that undergraduate training be as non-
technical as possible. I would urge that the best training
for subsequent graduate work in planning would be a broad
cultural liberal arts training. It should be heavy in those
subjects that give a student an appreciation of people and
ideas. I would add one more ingredient in the liberal arts
training, namely a pretty heavy dose of economics. It has
always been appalling to me to find out how little most planners
know about simple economic laws.

"My premise here is that the technical tools and the mechanical
devices will be given our young planners in graduate school. By
this time, the student with the broad cultural undergraduate
training will be in a position to know how to use what he has
at hand. He will understand both the possibilities and the
limitations of planning, and there are plenty of both. The
world is full of frustrated planners who are frustrated not
because they are incapable of devising very good schemes but
because they don't have the slightest idea about how to get
those schemes into the consciousness of the people and hence
into use."

117

2. From a lawyer – planner – teacher:

"With regard to the old 'specialist-generalist' controversy, I
am inclined to believe that better·results will be attained at
the undergraduate level through specialization in a particular
field, rather than general preparation. It seems to me that
perhaps the most important objective of undergraduate education
is the building of mental discipline and work habits which will
enable the student to plow through to the end of a difficult
problem. It is difficult to achieve this objective with a
broadly diffused course selection. Furthermore, the experience
of securing a thorough knowledge of one field will probably
serve as an anchor to which he can tie as he enters the broader
graduate level training.

"On the other hand, I think that it would be a mistaken idea to
insist that all planning students have the same background. There
is no doubt that the planner becomes perforce a 'generalist' at
some stage of his career, and he will benefit at that time from
having had contact with representatives of a variety of disciplines. By coming into contact with well-trained representatives
(i.e., the specialists we have been talking about), the student
will probably be better prepared than if he and all his fellows
had dabbled in a variety of fields while following a set 'pre-
planning' program.

"As to the specific fields from which planning students should be
drawn, I have no very strong convictions. It, no doubt, is helpful to the student to have majored in architecture, public administration, civil engineering, sociology, economics, or political
science. As a teacher, of course, it would save me time if the
student chose at least some of his electives with city planning
in mind. For instance, I find that most of my students are very
weak in their knowledge of local government (a weakness that is
general throughout our society); it would ease my task if they
were required to have at least some rudimentary knowledge thereof.
But I save even more time by having a class of students with
alert, well-trained minds which have been accustomed to digging
into a problem and grasping its essentials quickly."

3. From the director of a redevelopment commission:

"It is very difficult to say what undergraduate training is most
suitable as a basis for formal education in planning. The practice
of planning seems to fall in three categories: research and analysis,
design, and administration. While these functions may be performed
by separate persons in larger cities, they frequently must be dis-
charged by a single individual in smaller communities.

"Planning requires a mature and comprehensive mind, and I am therefore opposed to undergraduate degrees in planning. My observation
indicates that graduate study in planning can be beneficial and
productive to persons of varied prior education and experience,
and that it is best to hold as the object of graduate training the

supplementing and rounding out of total training and experience.
A person trained for planning should have some knowledge and compe-
tence in design, municipal engineering, research and analysis,
public administration, and law, and his graduate training should
be programmed to strengthen the aspects in which he is the weakest."

4. From the director of a social science institute:

"To me, the most important preparation is that the student make a
decision by his junior year that he intends to take graduate training in city planning. With so few schools offering a planning
curriculum and in view of the apparent lack of interest or knowledge
of city planning on the part of the teaching faculty in a large
number of our southern universities, there has been little or no
opportunity for a student to evidence an interest in planning as
a profession. Consequently graduate schools find they must 'retread'
a large number of their students who just 'happened' on city planning.
However, if the undergraduate student has decided to train for the
planning profession, he can select courses during his undergraduate
training to give him basic preparation both academically and mentally
for graduate training in planning. I do not feel that special pre-
paratory curricula are necessary. Nearly every school has enough
courses in its curriculum that will give a satisfactory basic preparation for graduate work in city planning."

The Dean of a College of Engineering reacted to these commentaries as
follows:

"It would appear from my observations that the city planners seem
anxious to keep their profession a closed one. So long as they
do this they will always have difficulty in finding a sufficient
supply of trained men to undertake graduate work in that field.
To make city planning an open profession, it seems to me that it
will be necessary to establish an undergraduate curriculum with
broad training that would lead to the advanced work in the graduate
field."

II

Committee Conclusions

The Committee agreed to accept the following basic assumptions:

1. The term "city planning" is intended to cover community, regional
and city planning.

2. City planning is a professional field that can be trained for.

3. Professional training in city planning should normally be at the
graduate level.

4. The graduate training program should draw from the social science
as well as from the design science fields.

are true, and the growing need for planners in the South, the high mor-

rate and the rapid staff turnover in planning offices remain unchanged,

ppears to be a real crisis at hand which the individual schools of city

g cannot cope with alone. There is need for concerted action by all

s concerned, public and private, to attract not only more but also a

caliber of student to the graduate schools already set up and prepared to

hem.

the field of city planning is relatively new, it is as yet unable to

on even terms with the well established professional curricula at the

e level. The breadth of subjects to be covered and the length of time

d in training tend to provide handicaps which must be offset.

III

Recommendations

ndation No. 1

e Regional Committee on City Planning establish a permanent coordinating

ittee on recruitment and undergraduate preparation, such sub-committee

at least one representative from each of the states supporting the

n Regional Education Board. The Committee believes that such a sub-committee

ost successfully undertake a number of inter-related activities which

be initiated and which will require a period of time to achieve desired

. It is further recommended that, since the graduate professional schools

planning accept qualified applicants with a bachelor's degree in such

s as architecture, civil engineering, landscape architecture, sociology,

cs, government, geography, and the humanities, and since nearly every

and university in the South has at least some of these courses in its

curricula, the sub-committee, working with professional societies, determine

le undergraduate "pre-planning" programs and inventory the courses now

le in southern institutions which would fit into such programs, the re-

o be incorporated in the pamphlet suggested below.

ndation No. 2

e Regional Committee on City Planning prepare, edit and publish an attract-

ustrated pamphlet which would set forth the prospects and potentials of a

in city planning as has already been done for forestry, to stimulate

t in city planning careers of potential professional students, those who

them in planning their undergraduate work, and the general public. This

t should be distributed by the Regional Committee to schools, colleges

versities in the States served by the Southern Regional Education Board.

ional Committee on City Planning might also give consideration to the use

r visual material such as films and slides by schools and other civic

to publicize careers in city planning.

ndation No. 3

mittee recommends the establishment of a centrally administered trust

c fellowships to be awarded to outstanding applicants to graduate planning

in the region. The acquisition of funds for scholarships and fellowships

f primary importance, the Committee believes that the sub-committee pro-

n Recommendation No. 1 might serve as a more effective instrument in se-

direct grants for graduate study than the several southern schools in

tion with each other. Funds for this purpose might be secured by a system-

npaign from sources such as:

   —individual donors
   —local as well as national business and industrial firms
   —civic groups
   —local, state and national agencies interested in obtaining a
       continuous supply of trained personnel
   —philanthropic foundations.

121

At the same time direct financial aid is being sought, the possibility of setting up undergraduate, on-the-job training programs might be examined by the sub-committee proposed above. This kind of assistance to the student could serve a less obvious but extremely valuable purpose in revealing natural aptitudes and providing a testing ground for fellowship applicants. Furthermore in the opinion of the Committee such on-the-job training, if taken prior to or alternating with college courses, would make the academic work far more meaningful.

A program similar to that being proposed has been in effect for many years at the University of Cincinnati. Both city and regional (county) planning commissions in the area have made effective use on their staffs of students in engineering, architecture and landscape architecture. The work has usually consisted of drafting or assistance in research, but in many cases students have been en-couraged to undertake graduate studies in city planning and have continued in that profession. Various other fields of undergraduate specialization pertinent to planning, such as sociology, public administration, and geography, might also be included under this kind of program. A much more generally applicable arrange-ment for on-the-job training is the use of undergraduate students, as well as graduate students, on planning commission staffs during the summer vacation.

A third method of stimulating interest of undergraduates in city planning through employment would be to utilize them in connection with appropriate planning commission projects — for example, engage them in a land-use survey as a part of a course in urban geography. The Committee believes that direct grants might be easier to obtain for schools showing some imagination and initiative in their own self-help projects.

122

Table 1

Per Cent of Cities over 50,000 pop. having Planning Staffs

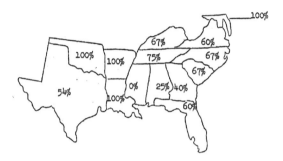

Per Cent of Cities over 25,000 pop. having Planning Staffs

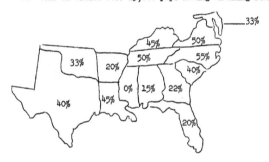

23 Cities over 50,000 pop. without Planning Staffs.
36 Cities over 50,000 pop. with Planning Staffs. 60%

80 Cities over 25,000 pop. without Planning Staffs.
41 Cities over 25,000 pop. with Planning Staffs. 30%

373 Cities in the Southeast have city managers.

CHAPTER XIII

SHORT—COURSE TRAINING IN CITY PLANNING

123

COMMITTEE ON SHORT COURSE TRAINING IN CITY PLANNING

<u>Committee Members</u>

T. Arnett, Dean
of Architecture and
d Arts
lty of Florida
lle, Florida

Jerral T. Harper, Regional Director
East Tennessee Office
Tennessee State Planning Commission
City Hall Park
Knoxville, Tennessee

Dulaney
oring
a

Jean Hillencamp, Clerk
Municipal Court of West Memphis
West Memphis, Arkansas

sser
te of Government
lty of North Carolina
Hill, North Carolina

J. Duval Lee
Planning Engineer
City Hall
Lynchburg, Virginia

William S. Bonner, <u>Chairman</u>
Acting Director
Social Science Research Division
Institute of Science and Technology
University of Arkansas
Fayetteville, Arkansas

124

REPORT

Purpose

The purpose of the Committee on Short-Course Training in City Planning was to
consider how best to meet the need for formal training courses of short duration
in the field of city planning. The Committee considered which groups should be
reached, who should conduct the training, and what types of training might be
undertaken.

I

Findings

There are primarily two groups which should be reached through short-course
training in city planning: employees of governmental units concerned with
planning functions in the performance of their duties, and members of local
planning commissions or boards. Members of professional and civic organizations interested in city development and growth can be oriented in planning
more effectively by means other than short-course training. The term "short-
course training" includes such devices as institutes, short courses, forums,
clinics, and workshops. They are formal in that they are scheduled occasions
directed toward a definite objective, whether it be general orientation or
specific technical or administrative problems. The duration of such training
may be a part of a day or a number of days over an extended period.

125

II

Committee Conclusions

The Committee believes that, although certain training activities may be conducted on the regional level, the primary responsibility for short-course
training should lie with the states. For two specific training activities,
however, a regional approach is suggested. The establishment of a method for
the exchange of information on short-course methods and content is one such
activity. This would assist the institutions and agencies sponsoring short-
course training by keeping them informed on the activities and programs being
undertaken. Regional meetings could be held for the purpose of discussing
course content, problems involved in developing courses, and the techniques and
materials used in the short courses.

The second training function that may be performed on a regional level is the
sponsorship of short-courses for members of planning staffs and planning administrators who have had little formal training in city planning. The training
may be best carried out on a region-wide or group-of-states basis. The Committee
suggests that the course last two weeks and have as its primary objective the
introduction of the individual to the basic subject matter of city planning.
Such a training course would be given in an academic setting with a faculty
drawn from the host institution and other institutions and agencies.

Although a varying amount of effort to conduct short-course training of some type
goes on in each of the 14 states, the Committee feels that some agency in each
of the states should sponsor and develop a continuing program. While an educational institution may be the desirable agency to furnish the impetus for a
training program, in many states other organizations of governmental officials
and of private citizens have taken an active role. This should be encouraged.

126

Whatever agency assumes responsibility for short-course training, the program should be expanded into a vital force in community education and development.

The program evolved in each state will no doubt be different, but any comprehensive program should seek to accomplish the following objectives:

1. Specialized training for local employees who require planning training in the performance of their duties.

2. General orientation instruction for all appointive or elective officials in planning responsibilities, principles, and techniques.

3. Specific instruction in planning problems of general interest to local employees and officials.

4. A means of interchanging ideas and experiences for solving planning problems.

5. Provision of each employee or official with text materials to guide him in the daily performance of his duties.

A variety of methods have been used successfully to achieve these objectives. If a conference of agencies engaged in short-course training in the 14-state area is called, as recommended below, the participants might prepare a comprehensive list of courses now being conducted, the subject matter of each course, and an evaluation of the way each type of course has met the above objectives, based on the experience of the states which have employed them. The officials or employees invited to a particular course will depend on the subject matter of the course. The two general types of courses might be outlined as follows:

1. Specialized instruction

a. In a state-wide school for a period of from one to three or more weeks.

b. At four or five locations in the state with weekly or bi-weekly meetings over a period of several months.

c. For interested employees and officials in a particular city with one or more meetings every one or two weeks over a period of several months. (Could be conducted using correspondence materials.)

127

2. General orientation instruction and instruction in specific planning problems

    a. In state-wide schools for a period of from one to five days.

    b. In a series of meetings in centrally-located cities (to which employees and officials of cities in each area would come) for a period of one or more days.

    c. At a meeting in a particular city for employees and officials of that city.

    d. At periodic conferences or seminars in one or more centrally-located cities for specific groups of officials or employees, such as city planners.

III

Recommendations

Recommendation No. 1

It is recommended that a method be developed by which information on short course training may be interchanged within the 14-state area, in order to encourage the development and expansion of short-course training in city planning. To develop such a method it is recommended that a meeting be called at which representatives of universities, agencies, and organizations which are interested in sponsoring short-course training can meet. This meeting could consider problems involved in developing short-courses, the content of short-courses and the techniques and materials used in them, and the desirability of a regional catalogue on short-courses. The meeting might also consider ways of encouraging institutions and agencies to meet specific needs for training in city planning. It is recommended that this meeting be sponsored by the Regional Committee on City Planning.

Recommendation No. 2

It is recommended that consideration be given the establishment of a training

center or centers in the 14-state area, in order to give members of planning
staffs and planning administrators who have had little training in city planning
an opportunity for supplemental training. The purpose of the center would be
to introduce the individuals to the basic subject matter of city planning in
a short course approximately two weeks long. It is further recommended that
the Regional Committee on City Planning survey the universities in the various
states to determine their interest in establishing such centers and to aid
those interested in developing a course of instruction to meet the needs.

COMMITTEE ON CASE MATERIAL IN CITY PLANNING

Committee Members

Brown
onville City Planning
isory Board
est Forsyth Street
onville, Florida

rd O. Niehoff, Chief
ing and Education Relations
ssee Valley Authority
ille, Tennessee

A. Norton
l of Public Administration
da State University
hassee, Florida

p A. Stedfast
tor of City Planning
Hall
bia, South Carolina

Seward Weber
Assistant Director of Planning
Department of Planning
City Hall
Greensboro, North Carolina

Max S. Wehrly
Executive Director
The Urban Land Institute
1737 K. Street, N. W.
Washington 6, D. C.

York Willbern, Head
Department of Political Science
University of Alabama
University, Alabama

Lawrence L. Durisch, Chairman
Chief of Government Research
Tennessee Valley Authority
Knoxville, Tennessee

130

REPORT

Purpose

The Committee on Case Materials in City Planning had as its purpose consideration
of the needs and utilization of records of planning situations as instructional
material for the training and information of planning commission members and staff
and interested citizens, and of possible methods of securing competent write-ups
and distribution of such material.

I

Findings

Case materials are descriptions of actual planning situations, prepared with a
view to giving readers a sense of participation in the planning process. They
are especially designed to serve educational needs. For the teacher they make
possible an examination of particulars as a supplement to the discussion of
general principles. Thus they do not stress generalization or theoretical
principles but supply instead a situation in which such principles may be discussed and tested. The material usually takes the form of a detailed narrative
account of how a problem in planning developed, how it was identified and classified for action, how and by whom the decisions relating to it were made, and how
a solution was worked out and carried into effect. Planning case materials provide opportunity for use of maps, diagrams and other graphic materials prepared
in the field. Case materials may cover both matters of policy and planning
techniques. They may include examples of both good and poor planning. They provide opportunity to illustrate the normal working out of problems as well as
situations in which there are abnormal, or at least unexpected, developments.

131

Case materials can, to a remarkable degree, give an understanding of the conditions under which planning problems are defined, pertinent data assembled, alternatives considered and decisions reached. Case material can also give an understanding of the consequences of a course of action followed in particular, well-described situations. They may also be used to illustrate the inter-relation of planning problems in a given city and the cumulative effect of planning actions. Case materials can show the breadth of agency and institutional participation in city planning, as well as the inter-disciplinary nature of the field.

Case material is already extensively used in instruction in city planning and by a few planning agencies for purposes of in-service training. On an informal basis case materials are also used for purposes of citizen education and for stimulating general interest in city planning.

II

Conclusions

There is need for more case materials on city planning in the South. Published journals, news letters and other current sources do not provide sufficient material of the type needed. Nor has there been sufficient orderly attention devoted to producing case materials. The development and methods of producing, distributing and promoting the utilization of case materials in city planning has been neglected. The Committee believes that considered attention given to the problem by an organization and staff devoted to that purpose will be success-ful in securing full and excellent cooperation from practitioners in the field.

The Committee believes the following purposes should be served by such case material:

Instruction in regular university classes and in short courses.

In-service education of practitioners of planning.

CHAPTER XIV

CASE MATERIALS IN CITY PLANNING

132

Education and information for "laymen" active in the field.

Material for the general public to be used by newspapers and other media of citizen education.

Professional development of the authors of case materials.

The production of case material in city planning must be recognized as an important project. First, city planning itself occupies a rather strategic area in the social science field. It is an area of special interest to students of political science and public administration due to the rapid development of institutions of urban government. The growth of cities and city problems are also of great current interest to sociologists, psychologists, social psychologists, economists and others. The production and distribution of significant case material in the field of city planning could serve very broad interests as well as those professional purposes somewhat more narrowly defined.

The establishment of a going program of production of case material, however small it might be and however inadequately it might cover such a large and complex field, would doubtless put a committee on case materials in a better position to seek adequate financing and organizational arrangements for a sustained program of production. The initial problem is clearly one of establishing a beginning from which more advanced steps can be taken.

III

Recommendations

It is recommended that a committee on case materials in city planning be established. Such a committee might well be organized by the Regional Committee on City Planning which has been established under the Southern Regional Education Compact. It is further recommended that arrangements be made for a junior faculty

member from one of the universities participating in the regional program to devote part time to the problem of producing case materials in city planning. Such
an arrangement for faculty time could be of great advantage to all of the schools
in the region offering instruction in city planning, and of possible assistance
in general curricula in political science and public administration, as well as
in courses in sociology and economics. The arrangement would, moreover, seem to
be very much in accord with the cooperative purposes and functions of the Regional
Committee on City Planning.

It is suggested that the committee be appointed and an individual secured to
begin work under its general direction without waiting to prepare a project for
foundation support or to seek special financing. The initial job might involve
the following activities:

1. Stimulation of the production of case materials chiefly by
   practitioners and teachers of planners. Some ingenious
   methods may need to be devised to help practitioners organize
   their time to do the necessary initial writing; student assistance may be helpful in easing the load of writing by teachers;
   some faculty time may need to be allocated for this specific
   purpose. But the time of experienced and articulate people
   must be found if the essential writing production is done.

2. The development of standards and techniques of reporting and
   editing case materials. Attention is called to the written
   instructions sent out by the Inter-University Case Program in
   Public Administration. These instructions are designed to interest individuals in preparing case material and to suggest
   form and content of acceptable studies. Something similar might
   be worked out by the faculty member mentioned above for the
   field of city planning.

3. The identification of case material which will be particularly
   useful in the early states of production and the solicitation,
   when necessary, of authors to write these cases. It will be
   necessary to assist in identifying case materials - and if
   balance is to be obtained, to suggest some of the lines along
   which material is needed for instructional and other purposes.

4. The working out of arrangements for the publication and distribution of the case materials. The publication and
   distribution arrangements for the separate cases of the Inter-
   University Program in Public Administration might be available
   and satisfactory for case materials in city planning.

134

If a regional journal in city planning is established, abbreviated cases might be utilized to make up one of its sections or departments. Longer cases could often be used as feature articles. Various newsletters already in existence carry a great deal of case material, but without any uniform style or method of presentation. However, news letters do contain clues as to valuable material which might be suitable for more formal case presentation.

These and other possible arrangements should be promptly explored by the proposed committee. Publication of case materials in book form might well be deferred until a fairly large number of separate cases have been prepared and tested in class work.

CHAPTER XV

CITIZEN. PARTICIPATION IN CITY PLANNING

135

COMMITTEE ON CITIZEN PARTICIPATION IN CITY PLANNING

Committee Members

rick H. Bair, Jr.
tary
da Planning and Zoning Association
ille, Florida

ret Breland
Planner
politan Planning Commission
ta, Georgia

Cowgill, Head
tment of Architecture
nia Polytechnic Institute
sburg, Virginia

Goodman
Manager
don, Virginia

James E. Pate
College of William and Mary
Williamsburg, Virginia

Ronald Scott
Director of Planning
Department of Planning
City Hall
Greensboro, North Carolina

Frank W. Ziegler
Nashville Chamber of Commerce
Nashville 3, Tennessee

Gerald Gimre, Chairman
Executive Director
Nashville Housing Authority
701 South Sixth Street
Nashville 6, Tennessee

136

REPORT

Purpose

The purpose of the Committee on Citizen Participation in City Planning was to explore the ways by which citizens in a community might, through systematic participation in the planning processes, help formulate basic planning policies, make basic planning decisions and obtain for their respective communities effective city planning commissions, competent professional assistance and the realization of well-laid city plans.

I

Findings

Citizen participation is action by any citizen or group of citizens outside the city officials who utilize an effective means of voicing their opinion on planning processes or on any segment of a city plan.

An examination of the planning processes in southern communities reveals that such citizen participation as has been accomplished has been spotty in extent and sporadic in character. There is little evidence to reveal any consistent program of citizen participation for any considerable period of time in any southern community. There are excellent examples of such participation for specific undertakings: activity to create a city planning commission, to adopt a zoning ordinance, to perfect a recreation plan or to solve other particular problems confronting the community. Yet we lack examples of consistent, long-term citizen participation in the planning programs of our southern cities.

137

II

Conclusions

The lack of adequate examples of citizen participation may, to some extent, be related to public indifference to all local governmental functions and processes. If citizens, in general, were more alert to the functions and operations of their local governments, the task of obtaining the participation of those same citizens in the processes of planning would be simpler and the results more effective.

The Committee is of the opinion that there needs to be an exploration of the subject in order to ascertain where citizen participation has been most successful even though it has not met the ideal goals of consistency and continuity. The failures of citizen participation should also be examined. With examples both good and bad, perhaps some general conclusions might be reached which citizens could use as a guide in obtaining effective action and competent planning in their localities.

The Committee debated whether or not citizen participation is needed, advisable or necessary in the planning processes.

There are those who are of the opinion that the citizen members of a city planning commission constitute citizen participation to the extent necessary. The unpaid, appointed members are thought to represent the general body of citizens, and to be able, along with elected officials, properly and adequately to plan, program and decide the planning needs of a given community, with or without technical assistance, depending to some extent on the size of the city.

The Committee feels, however, that city planning is more than a routine function of city government. By its very nature, city planning undertakes programs

which affect the lives and property of its citizens in more ways than do those of
the operating branches of city government. The parts of a city plan which control the design and layout of unplotted lands, the plans for widening or extending roads or highways, the effective control of the uses of lands, the designs
for the location of recreation areas or the preparation of a capital budget program, touch and affect so many citizens in a direct and personal way as to require all the citizens to participate in the processes of policy making, and the
creation, design and effectuation of the city plan.

III

Recommendations

Recommendation No. 1

The Committee recommends that the Regional Committee on City Planning consider
undertaking a study of the outstanding examples of citizen participation in city
planning and the publication of the results thereof as a guide which citizens
may consult.

The Committee is aware that effective citizen participation will vary in nature
from city to city. There are many customary methods of obtaining citizen participation such as through citizens' planning councils, chambers of commerce,
newspapers or special publications, or through many other sources of assistance,
depending on the city. It is because participation by such means or through
other processes is not generally known that the Committee has made its recommendation.

ndation No. 2

nittee recommends that citizen participation should be effectuated in

t three points in the planning process:

The citizens of any community should join in determining
the opportunities for development and the needs.

Citizens should assist in the selection of objectives from
among alternative courses of action.

Citizens should assist in the attainment of the planning
objectives.

eves, however, that citizen groups or organizations should not attempt to

the administrative functions or the duly constituted powers of an official

g commission.

dation No. 3

uittee recommends that the Regional Committee on City Planning sponsor

ngresses on City Planning in the South and that broader citizen parti-

in such congresses be encouraged.

congresses could be held and if there could be brought about a partici-

y citizens interested in city planning, together with municipal officials,

uld be comparison, experience and guidance set forth in such manner as

er a program for competent city planning in our southern cities.

A P P E N D I X

ROSTER OF DELEGATES TO

THE SOUTHERN REGIONAL CONGRESS ON CITY PLANNING

Name	Delegate of
...iam T. Arnett, Dean ...ege of Architecture and ...lied Arts ...ersity of Florida ...esville, Florida	University of Florida
...y B. Augur ...n Vulnerability Specialist ...ce of Defense Mobilization ...utive Office of the President ...ington 25, D. C.	Office of Defense Mobilization
...swick A. Bagdon ...onal Director ...au of Labor Statistics ... Department of Labor ...eventh Street, N. E. ...nta 5, Georgia	Bureau of Labor Statistics U. S. Department of Labor
...erick H. Bair, Jr. ...etary ...ida Planning and Zoning ...sociation ...ille, Florida	Florida Planning and Zoning Association
...ard L. Beck ...utive Director ... of Roanoke Redevelopment and ...using Authority ... Box 1807 ...ke, Virginia	Roanoke Redevelopment and Housing Authority
...s C. Bisso, Director ... Planning and Zoning ...mission of the City of ...w Orleans ...d Annex ...t. Charles Street ...rleans 12, Louisiana	City Planning and Zoning Commission of the City of New Orleans
...am S. Bonner ...ng Director ...l Science Research Division ...tute of Science and Technology ...teville, Arkansas	University of Arkansas
...ret Breland ...Planner ...politan Planning Commission ...rand Building ...ta, Georgia	Metropolitan Planning Commission
... Brown ...orville City Planning ...sory Board ...est Forsyth Street ...onville, Florida	Jacksonville City Planning Advisory Board

ame	Delegate of
Brown, Assistant Director unty Research Foundation ropolitan Building E. Second Avenue Florida	Dade County Research Foundation
uchanan ant on Highway Economics n Regional Education Board t Peachtree Street, N. E. Georgia	Southern Regional Education Board
ullock, Head ent of Sociology outhern University , Texas	Texas Southern University
t Carroll, Planner Bartholomew and Associates 11 , Georgia	Harland Bartholomew and Associates
Carter ve Director unty Planning and Zoning ssion 11 , Georgia	City-County Planning and Zoning Commission
rt Chapin, Jr. te Professor ent of City and Regional ing ty of North Carolina iill, North Carolina	University of North Carolina
, Chapin Faculties Institute of Technology , Georgia	———
P. Clayton, Head tern Office Bartholomew and Associates etta Street Building 3, Georgia	Harland Bartholomew and Associates
ok, Director unty Planning Board lorida	Dade County Planning Board
ooper, Associate Director f Public Administration da ty of Virginia esville, Virginia	University of Virginia

Name	Delegate of
owgill, Head ent of Architecture a Polytechnic Institute urg, Virginia	Virginia Polytechnic Institute
Creese . Hite Art Museum ity of Louisville lle 8, Kentucky	University of Louisville
R. Darragh, Manager n Division l Association of Manuracturers ring Street, N. W. , Georgia	Southern Division National Association of Manu- facturers
L. Daugherty t Paces Ferry Road, N. E. , Georgia	Edward L. Daugherty
Davis, Vice President a Transit Association th David Street d 20, Virginia	American Transit Association
W. Dibble W. Dibble and Company ants h Main Street South Carolina	Wortham W. Dibble and Company
H. Dill, Director re County Planning Commission hington Avenue 4, Maryland	Baltimore County Planning Commission
Dinwiddie, Dean of Architecture University eans, Louisiana	Tulane University
. Dolbeare, Vice President relopment a Electric Power Company 9, Virginia	Virginia Electric and Power Company
Dulaney ring, Virginia	Paul S. Dulaney
L. Durisch Government Research of Regional Studies e Valley Authority e, Tennessee	Tennessee Valley Authority

me	Delegate of

sser, Assistant Director
e of Government
ty of North Carolina
ill, North Carolina

Institute of Government
University of North Carolina

P. Farnsley

City of Louisville

le, Kentucky

ss, Chief
and Engineering Branch
of Slum Clearance and Urban
lopment
and Home Finance Agency
on 25, D. C.

Housing and Home Finance Agency

ora, Chairman
City Planning Commission
ood Avenue
, South Carolina

Columbia City Planning Commission

elius
nning Commission
l
ity, Missouri

Western Electric Company
Winston-Salem, North Carolina

n Francis
nner III
State Planning Board
ch Street
ry 4, Alabama

Alabama State Planning Board

Robert T. Fuller, Chief
Requirements Branch
Division
f the Chief of Civil
s and Military Government
agon
on 25, D. C.

Office of the Chief of Civil
Affairs and Military Government
Department of the Army

. Gant
Committee on City Planning
nt for Graduate Programs
Regional Education Board
Peachtree Street, N. W.
Georgia

Southern Regional Education Board

imre, Executive Director
e Housing Authority
h Sixth Street
e 6, Tennessee

Nashville Housing Authority

odman
ager
, Virginia

Abingdon, Virginia

Name	Delegate of
R. Grand, Head ent of Architecture of Architecture and Allied Arts ity of Florida lle, Florida	University of Florida
J. Gray ommunity Planner ent Research Branch ee Valley Authority le, Tennessee	Tennessee Valley Authority
P. Green, Jr. nt Director te of Government ity of North Carolina ill, North Carolina	Institute of Government University of North Carolina
Kammer ve Officer ee of the South l Planning Association n Building Georgia	Committee of the South
C. Harper, Regional Director nnessee Office ee State Planning Commission l Park e, Tennessee	East Tennessee Office Tennessee State Planning Commission
W. Hawkins of Development e Housing Authority h Sixth Street e 6, Tennessee	Nashville Housing Authority
T. Hedden and Zoning Consultant 14th Street, N. E. Georgia	Paul van T. Hedden
. Highsaw, Director f Public Administration ty of Mississippi ty, Mississippi	University of Mississippi
. Hill, Chairman nt of Sociology University tnut Street, S. W. Georgia	Atlanta University
lencamp, Clerk l Court of West Memphis phis, Arkansas	City Planning Commission

Name	Delegate of
Hinds, Regional Director nnessee Office ee State Planning Commission , Tennessee	West Tennessee Office Tennessee State Planning Commission
on Hoffman on Hoffman, Inc. g Consultants syth Building , Georgia	John Leon Hoffman, Inc.
. Holder ial and Industrial Real Estate e Building 3, Georgia	Southern Industrial Development Council
. Hubley, Jr. ve Director ural and Industrial ment Board tol Office Building t, Kentucky	Kentucky Agricultural and Industrial Development Board
Ivey, Jr., Director a Regional Education Board Peachtree Street, N. W. Georgia	Southern Regional Education Board
James, Executive Secretary Planning and Civic Association n Trust Building on 5, D. C.	American Planning and Civic Association
James, Director n Division ve Safety Foundation Building on 6, D. C.	Automotive Safety Foundation
Kamphoefner, Dean f Design rolina State College North Carolina	North Carolina State College
H. Kraft, Chief of Local Planning nt of Conservation and pment e Finance Building 19, Virginia	Department of Conservation and Development
Kyle t Professor of Education of Education ty of Oklahoma Oklahoma	University of Oklahoma

Name	Delegate of
awson, Manager ty and Rural Life Development tment arolina Electric and Gas Company a, South Carolina	South Carolina Electric and Gas Company
H. Leach ssociate n Regional Education Board t Peachtree Street, N. W. , Georgia	Southern Regional Education Board
l Lee, Planning Engineer ll rg, Virginia	League of Virginia Municipalities
ipziger-Pearce Director of Architecture ity of Texas 12, Texas	University of Texas
Lepawsky, Professor ent of Political Science ity of Alabama ity, Alabama	University of Alabama
M. Lester, Secretary e Corporation of New York ro Road Hill, North Carolina	Carnegie Corporation of New York
G. Little, Jr. nt Professor of Architecture Institute of Technology , Georgia	Georgia Institute of Technology
R. Locke anning Engineer anning Commission t Plume Street 10, Virginia	Norfolk City Planning Commission
Logan l Committee on City Planning r te of Community Development ity of Oklahoma Oklahoma	University of Oklahoma
V. Long, Commissioner and g Director ent of Conservation and opment te Finance Building d, Virginia	Department of Conservation and Development

Name	Delegate of
A. Lufburrow	Georgia Department of Commerce
al Representative	
Department of Commerce	
e Capitol	
Georgia	
Aden, Jr.	The Municipal South
ditorial Director	
x 1225	
e 1, North Carolina	
W. Meisenhelder, III	University of Tennessee
nt on Municipal Management	
al Technical Advisory Service	
e, Tennessee	
Menhinick	Georgia Institute of Technology
Committee on City Planning	
Professor of City Planning	
f Architecture	
Institute of Technology	
Georgia	
Miller	Appalachian Electric Power Co.
al Development Agent	
ian Electric Power Co.	
lin Road	
Virginia	
Miller	Tennessee State Planning Commission
Committee on City Planning	
e Director	
e State Planning Commission	
erce Street	
e, Tennessee	
Moore	City-County Planning Board
of Planning	Winston-Salem
nty Planning Board	
Salem, North Carolina	
Neal, Director	Tuskegee Institute
fe Council	
Institute	
Institute, Alabama	
O. Niehoff, Chief	Tennessee Valley Authority
and Education Relations	
e Valley Authority	
e, Tennessee	
Norton	Florida State University
f Public Administration	
State University	
see, Florida	

Name	Delegate of
3. Owens nager al Building Virginia	City of Roanoke
3. Owens, Chairman ent of Landscape Architecture ty of Georgia Georgia	University of Georgia
'Harrow te Director 1 Society of Planning Officials st 60th Street 37, Illinois	American Society of Planning Officials
t. Pappas Officer sources Research Institute rersity States Air Force Air Force Base, Alabama	Human Resources Research Institute
Parker Committee on City Planning partment of City and Regional ng ty of North Carolina ill, North Carolina	University of North Carolina
Pate of William and Mary burg, Virginia	College of William and Mary
L. Pickens, Dean f Architecture on University s 5, Missouri	Washington University
ratt l Director AND SENTINEL Salem, North Carolina	Winston-Salem JOURNAL-SENTINEL
F. Schumann, Jr. of Planning County Virginia	Virginia Citizens Planning Association
cott of Planning nt of Planning 1 ro, North Carolina	Greensboro Department of Planning

Name	Delegate of
mmons ille City Planning Advisory y Building Department ille, Florida	Jacksonville City Planning Advisory Board
L. Slayton, Assistant Director l Association of Housing ials enteenth Street, N. W. ton 6, D. C.	National Association of Housing Officials
ward Smith (Mrs. James M.) f Secretariat n Regional Education Board t Peachtree Street, N. W. , Georgia	
Smith, Director unty Planning Commission l1 a, Georgia	Cobb County Planning Commission
A. Stedfast r of City Planning l1 a, South Carolina	Columbia City Planning Commission
teinberg, Dean of Engineering ty of Maryland Park, Maryland	University of Maryland
L. Steiner, Director e Redevelopment Commission nicipal Building re 2, Maryland	Baltimore Redevelopment Commission
S. Sugg, Jr. sociate Regional Education Board Peachtree Street, N. W. Georgia	Southern Regional Education Board
. Tarrant ng City Planner 31st Street 25, Virginia	Julian W. Tarrant
Terrett and Housing Officer of Columbia Redevelopment gency sylvania Avenue, N. W. on 4, D. C.	District of Columbia Redevelopment Land Agency

Name	Delegate of
. Topp oning Inspector Miami Beach ll each, Florida	City of Miami Beach
allace nt to the Vice President Power Company etta Street, N. W. , Georgia	Georgia Power Company
len Ward rk, Florida	Mary Ellen Ward
. Webb te Professor ent of City and Regional Planning ity of North Carolina Hill, North Carolina	University of North Carolina
Weber nt Director of Planning ent of Planning ll oro, North Carolina	Department of Planning
rly, Executive Director an Land Institute Street, N. W. ton 6, D. C.	The Urban Land Institute
Whitlow, Jr. l Director ast Tennessee Office ee State Planning Commission al Building City, Tennessee	Upper East Tennessee Office Tennessee State Planning Commission
lbern of Public Administration ity of Alabama ty, Alabama	Southern Regional Training Program in Public Administration
Wood anner anning Commission rnor Street 19, Virginia	City Planning Commission
iott Wood nning Consultant Main Street h City, North Carolina	John Elliott Wood

Name	Delegate of
borough ommissioner , Planning Zoning Building sion lorida	City of Miami
Ziegler e Chamber of Commerce e 3, Tennessee	Nashville Chamber of Commerce
itzmann and Zoning Consultant ural and Industrial Development tol Office Building t, Kentucky	Kentucky Municipal League and Southern Association of State Planning and Development Agencies
uber Director Regional Congress on City Planning t Director itan Planning Commission n Building Georgia